1001 ESSENTIAL SENTENCES
FOR ELEMENTARY ENGLISH LEARNERS

CEDU 쎄듀는 A **C**omprehensive **E**nglish e**DU**cation(종합적 영어교육)의 약자입니다.

펴낸이	김기훈 · 김진희
펴낸곳	(주)쎄듀 / 서울시 강남구 논현로 305 (역삼동)
발행일	2016년 11월 28일 초판 1쇄
내용문의	www.cedubook.com
구입문의	콘텐츠 마케팅 사업본부
	Tel. 02-6241-2007
	Fax. 02-2058-0209
등록번호	제 22-2472호
ISBN	978-89-6806-079-3

초 등 코 치

천일문
sentence

세이펜과
초등코치 천일문 Sentence의 만남!

✦ ✦ ✦

〈초등코치 천일문 Sentence〉는 세이펜이 적용된 도서입니다.
세이펜을 영어에 가져다 대기만 하면 원어민이 들려주는 생생한 영어 발음과
억양을 바로 확인할 수 있습니다.

*세이펜은 본 교재에 포함되어 있지 않습니다.
기존에 보유하신 세이펜이 있다면 핀파일만 다운로드해서 바로 이용하실 수 있습니다.
단, Role-Play 기능은 SBS-1000 이후 모델에서만 구동됩니다.

초등코치 천일문 시리즈
with 세이펜

원어민 음성 실시간 반복학습	녹음 기능으로 쉐도잉 발음교정	게임 기능으로 재미있고 유익하게	Role-Play로 자신감까지 Up

초등코치 천일문 시리즈 Sentence 1권~5권, Grammar 1권~3권, Voca&Story 1권~2권 모두
세이펜을 활용하여 원어민 MP3 음성 재생 서비스를 이용할 수 있습니다.

(책 앞면 하단에 세이펜 로고 SAYPEN TV 가 있습니다.)

세이펜 핀파일 다운로드 안내

STEP ① 세이펜과 컴퓨터를 USB 케이블로 연결하세요.

STEP ② 쎄듀북 홈페이지(www.cedubook.com)에 접속 후, 학습자료실 메뉴에서 학습할 교재를 찾아 이동합니다.

> 초·중등교재 ▶ 구문 ▶ 학습교재 클릭 ▶ 세이펜 핀파일 자료 클릭
> ▶ 다운로드 (저장을 '다른 이름으로 저장'으로 변경하여 저장소를 USB로 변경) ▶ 완료

STEP ③ 음원 다운로드가 완료되면 세이펜과 컴퓨터의 USB 케이블을 분리하세요.

STEP ④ 세이펜을 분리하면 "시스템을 초기화 중입니다. 잠시만 기다려 주세요" 라는 멘트가 나옵니다.

STEP ⑤ 멘트 종료 후 세이펜을 〈초등코치 천일문 Sentence〉 표지의 제목 부분에 대보세요.
효과음이 나온 후 바로 학습을 시작할 수 있습니다.

참고사항

◆ 세이펜에서 제작된 모든 기종(기존에 보유하고 계신 기종도 호환 가능)으로 사용이 가능합니다. 단, Sentence 교재의 Role-Play 기능은
레인보우 SBS-1000 기종에서만 구동됩니다. (신규 구매자는 SBS-1000 이후 모델의 구매를 권장합니다.)

◆ 모든 기종은 세이펜에서 권장하는 최신 펌웨어 업데이트를 진행해 주시기 바랍니다.
업데이트는 세이펜 홈페이지(www.saypen.com)에서 가능합니다.

◆ 초등코치 천일문 시리즈의 핀파일은 쎄듀북 홈페이지(www.cedubook.com)와 세이펜 홈페이지(www.saypen.com)에서
모두 다운로드 가능합니다.

◆ 세이펜을 이용하지 않는 학습자는 쎄듀북 홈페이지 부가학습자료, 교재 내 QR코드 이미지 등을 활용하여 원어민 음성으로
학습하실 수 있습니다.

◆ 기타 문의사항은 www.cedubook.com / 02-3272-4766으로 연락 바랍니다.

초 등 코 치

천일문
sentence

✦ ✦ ✦

4

저자

김기훈　現 ㈜ 쎄듀 대표이사
　　　　現 메가스터디 영어영역 대표강사
　　　　前 서울특별시 교육청 외국어 교육정책자문위원회 위원
　　저서　천일문 / 천일문 Training Book / 천일문 GRAMMAR / 초등코치 천일문
　　　　어법끝 / 어휘끝 / 첫단추 / 쎈쓰업 / 파워업 / 빈칸백서 / 오답백서
　　　　쎄듀 본영어 / 문법의 골든룰 101 / ALL씀 서술형 / 수능실감
　　　　거침없이 Writing / Grammar Q / Reading Q / Listening Q
　　　　왓츠 그래머 / 왓츠 리딩 / 패턴으로 말하는 초등 필수 영단어 등

쎄듀 영어교육 연구센터
쎄듀 영어교육센터는 영어 콘텐츠에 대한 전문지식과 경험을 바탕으로
최고의 교육 콘텐츠를 만들고자 최선의 노력을 다하는 전문가 집단입니다.

인지영 책임연구원 · **장혜승** 선임연구원

검토위원

성윤선　現 Charles G. Emery Elementary School 교사
　　약력　하버드대학교 교육대학원 Language and Literacy 석사
　　　　이화여자대학교 교육공학, 영어교육 복수 전공
　　　　가톨릭대학교 교수학습센터 연구원
　　　　이화여자대학교 교수학습개발원 연구원
　　　　한국교육개발원 연구원

마케팅　　　콘텐츠 마케팅 사업본부
영업　　　　문병구
제작　　　　정승호
인디자인 편집　올댓에디팅
표지 디자인　윤혜영
내지 디자인　에피그램
영문교열　　Eric Scheusner

Foreword

〈초등코치 천일문 SENTENCE〉 시리즈를 펴내며

초등 영어, 무엇을 어떻게 시작해야 할까요?

자녀에게 영어 공부를 시키는 목적은 여러 가지일 것입니다. '우리 아이가 원어민처럼 영어를 잘했으면 좋겠다', '생활하는 데 영어가 걸림돌이 되지 않으면 좋겠다'라는 바람에서, 또는 중학교 내신이나 대학 입시를 위해 영어 공부를 시키기도 하지요.

영어를 공부하는 목표가 무엇이 되든, 영어의 기초가 잡혀 있지 않으면 새로운 것을 배우는 데 시간과 노력이 더 많이 들 수밖에 없습니다. 그리고 영어는 아이가 공부해야 하는 단 하나의 과목이 아니기에, 영어 공부에 비교적 많은 시간을 투자할 수 있는 초등학생 시기가 매우 중요하지요.

〈초등코치 천일문 SENTENCE〉 시리즈는 기초를 세우기에 가장 적절한 초등학생 시기에 **1,001개 통문장 암기로 영어의 기초를 완성**할 수 있도록 기획되었습니다. 1,001개 문장은 꼭 알아야 할 패턴 112개와 실생활에 유용한 표현들로 구성되었습니다.

| 문장과 덩어리 표현(chunk)이 학습의 주가 됩니다.

영어를 학습할 때는 문장(full sentence)과 덩어리 표현(chunk) 학습법이 더욱 효과적입니다. 〈초등코치 천일문 SENTENCE〉는 우리말 설명을 최소화하고 문장 자체에 집중할 수 있도록 구성했습니다. 책에 수록된 모든 문장과 표현, 대화는 現 미국 공립 초등학교 선생님의 검토를 받아 완성되었습니다.

| 문장 암기를 쉽게 할 수 있도록 설계했습니다.

문장과 표현이 자연스럽게 7번 반복되어 책을 따라 하다 보면 자동으로 1,001개 문장을 암기할 수 있습니다. 그리고 이해와 기억을 돕기 위해 재미있는 그림으로 새로운 표현들과 상황을 제시했습니다. 또한, 대부분 문장의 주어를 '나(I)'로 하여 아이들이 실생활에서도 자주 말하고 쓸 수 있도록 했습니다.

1,001개 통문장 암기로 탄탄한 기초가 세워지면, 내신, 수능, 말하기·듣기 등 앞으로의 모든 영어 학습에 대한 불안감이 해소될 것입니다. 〈초등코치 천일문 SENTENCE〉 시리즈와의 만남을 통해 영어 학습이 더욱더 쉬워지고 즐거워지는 경험을 꼭 할 수 있기를 희망합니다.

저 자

추천의 글

외국어 학습은 수년의 시간이 수반되는 장거리 경주입니다. 따라서, 잘못된 방식으로 학습을 시작해 외국어 학습의 즐거움을 초반에 잃어버리면, 끝까지 지속하지 못하고 중도에 포기하게 됩니다. 쎄듀의 초등코치 천일문은 대한민국의 초등 영어 학습자들이 효과적이고 효율적으로 영어학습의 경주를 시작할 수 있도록 여러분의 걸음을 친절하고 꼼꼼하게 안내해 줍니다.

효과적인 초등 영어 학습을 약속합니다.

영어 학습 과정에서 단어를 하나하나 익히는 것도 물론 중요하지만, 덩어리(chunk) 또는 패턴으로 다양한 영어 표현을 익히면 영어를 보다 유창하게 구사하고, 빠른 속도로 이해할 수 있습니다. 쎄듀의 초등코치 천일문은 일상 생활에서 가장 빈번히 사용되는 112개의 문장 패턴을 담았습니다.

또한, 각 문장 패턴당 8~9개의 훈련 문장들과 함께 4개의 짧은 대화가 수록되어 해당 패턴을 실제로 어떻게 사용할 수 있는지 보여줍니다. 이렇게 다양한 예문과 구체적인 대화 상황을 제시함으로써 쎄듀 초등코치 천일문은 언어 학습에 필수적인 패턴을 활용한 반복 학습을 이루어 갑니다.

112개의 필수 영어 문장 패턴과 이를 활용한 1,001개의 예문 학습, 그리고 구석구석 꼼꼼하게 안내된 어휘 학습까지. 쎄듀의 초등코치 천일문은 영어 학습을 시작하는 학생들이 탄탄한 영어의 기초를 다질 수 있는 효과적인 학습방법을 제시합니다.

효율적인 초등 영어 학습을 약속합니다.

애써 영어 공부를 했는데, 실제 영어를 사용하는 현장에서 활용할 수 없다면 어떻게 해야 할까요? 기존의 학습 내용을 지우고, 출발점으로 돌아가 다시 시작해야 합니다. 장거리를 달려야 하는데 다시 시작이라니 지칠 수밖에 없습니다.

쎄듀의 초등코치 천일문은 한 문장 한 문장, 대화 하나하나를 미국 초등학생들이 실제로 사용하는지 철저히 고려하여 엄선된 내용을 채택하였습니다. 초등학생들의 관심 주제를 바탕으로 문장과 대화들이 작성되어 학습자 모두 내용을 친숙하게 느낄 수 있습니다.

친숙한 대화 소재를 바탕으로 한 실제적인 영어 예문 학습을 통해, 본 교재를 이용한 학생들은 잘못된 공부로 인한 소진 없이 효율적으로 영어의 기본기를 다질 수 있습니다.

LA에서, 성윤선

Series

초등코치 천일문 SENTENCE〉 시리즈 구성

1권 Track 01~24 001-212	2권 Track 25~48 213-428	3권 Track 49~70 429-624	4권 Track 71~91 625-813	5권 Track 92~112 814-1001
This is ~.	I can ~.	I'm going to ~.	I started -ing.	Give me ~.
That's ~.	I can't ~.	He[She]'s going to ~.	I began to ~.	He[She] gave me ~.
I am a/an ~.	You can ~.	Are you going to ~?	Stop -ing.	I'll show you ~.
I am ~.	Can I ~?	I was about to ~.	I[We] kept -ing.	I'll tell you ~.
I'm not ~.	Can you ~?	I'm -ing.	I want to ~.	It makes me ~.
You are ~.	I[You] should ~.	He[She]'s -ing.	I don't want to ~.	He[She, It] made me ~.
He[She] is ~.	You must ~.	Are you -ing?	I wanted to ~.	Let me ~.
He[She] is in ~.	I[You] might ~.	I was -ing.	I like to ~.	Help me ~.
It is ~.	I have to ~.	What's ~?	I need to ~.	I want you to ~.
Are you ~?	You have to ~.	What do you ~?	I tried to ~.	I saw him[her] -ing.
It's ~.	You don't have to ~.	What are you -ing?	I'm supposed to ~.	I heard him[her] -ing.
There is ~.	I had to ~.	Who is ~?	It's time to ~.	I think (that) ~.
There are ~.	I used to ~.	Why do you ~?	Do you know how to ~?	I don't think (that) ~.
Is[Are] there any ~?	I was ~.	Why don't we ~?	I don't know what to ~.	I thought (that) ~.
There's no ~.	He[She] was ~.	Where is ~?	He[She] seems to ~.	I know (that) ~.
I have ~.	I went to ~.	Where did you ~?	You look ~.	I knew (that) ~.
He[She] has ~.	I put it ~.	How do you ~?	I feel ~.	I don't know what ~.
I want ~.	I didn't ~.	When are you going to ~?	I got ~.	I guess (that) ~.
I like ~.	Did you ~?	What a[an] ~!	I'm getting ~.	I hope (that) ~.
I hate ~.	I[We] will ~.	Do[Be] ~.	He[She] seems ~.	I'm sure (that) ~.
I need ~.	He[She] will ~.	Don't ~.	It looks like ~.	That's why ~.
I don't ~.	I won't ~.	Let's ~.		
Do you ~?	I'll be able to ~.			
Does he[she] ~?	Will you ~?			

Preview

Step 1

대표 문장과 패턴을 확인합니다.

미국 도서관 협회 추천 영어 동화책을 분석하여 가장 많이 쓰이는 패턴 112가지를 쉽고 간략한 설명과 함께 여러 예문으로 제시했습니다.

QR코드

휴대폰을 통해 QR 코드를 인식하면, 본문의 모든 문장, 단어 및 청크, 대화의 MP3 파일이 재생됩니다.

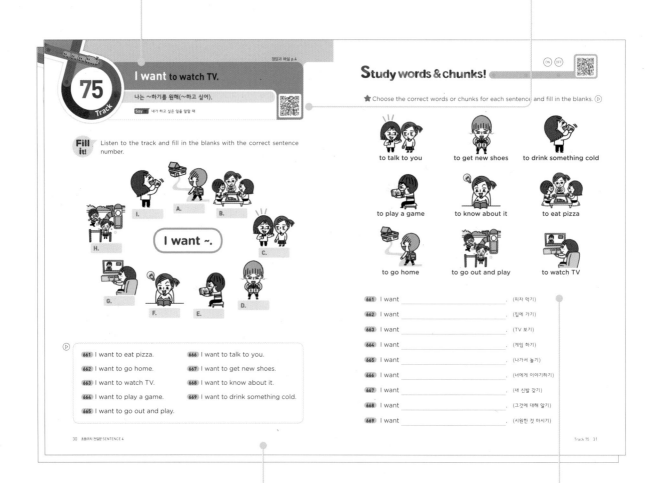

Step 2

미국 현지 초등학생 원어민 성우들이 읽는 문장들을 듣고 그림과 연결합니다.

귀로 듣고 눈으로 보면서 직접 패턴과 청크들을 연결합니다. 보기와 듣기까지 동시에 함으로써 학습 내용을 오래 기억할 수 있습니다.

Step 3

단어와 청크를 집중적으로 연습합니다.

단어와 청크 뜻에 맞는 그림을 연결해 보면서 문장을 완성합니다. 실생활에서 자주 쓸 수 있는 유용한 표현들을 익힐 수 있습니다.

Step 4

각 그림 상황에 알맞은 문장을 완성합니다.

앞에서 배운 패턴과 청크를 사용하여 완전한 문장을 써 봅니다. 재미있는 그림을 통해 문장이 실제로 사용되는 상황을 알 수 있습니다.

Step 5

각 대화 상황에 알맞은 문장을 넣어 봅니다.

학습한 문장이 실제로 어떤 대화 상황에서 쓰일 수 있는지 확실하게 알 수 있습니다.

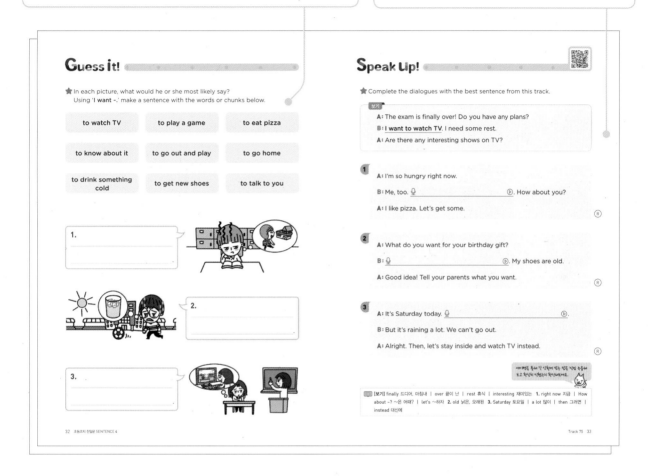

Step 6

워크북으로 단어 및 청크, 문장을 마스터합니다.

Step 7

무료 부가서비스 자료로 완벽하게 복습합니다.

1. 어휘리스트 2. 어휘테스트 3. 본문 해석 연습지
4. 본문 말하기·영작 연습지   5. MP3 파일

* 모든 자료는 www.cedubook.com에서 다운로드 가능합니다.

MP3 활용하기

〈초등코치 천일문 SENTENCE〉 부가서비스 자료에는 본문의 모든 문장, 단어 및 청크, 대화의 MP3 파일이 들어 있습니다.

• 미국 현지 초등학생 원어민 성우의 생생하고 정확한 발음과 억양을 확인할 수 있습니다.
• 문장은 2회씩 녹음되어 있습니다.

Strong Points

1 20일 또는 16일 완성

〈초등코치 천일문 SENTENCE〉 시리즈는 한 권을 20일 또는 16일 동안 학습할 수 있도록 구성되어 있습니다. 아이의 상황에 맞게 계획표를 선택하여 학습할 수 있습니다.

2 복잡한 문법 설명 없이도 가능한 학습

어렵고 복잡한 문법 용어를 설명할 필요가 없습니다. 패턴과 문장 자체의 의미를 받아들이는 데 집중하도록 구성되어 부담 없이 학습해 나갈 수 있습니다.

3 문장이 자연스럽게 외워지는 자동 암기 시스템

각 트랙에는 8~9개의 문장이 수록되어 있습니다. 본책과 워크북에는 이러한 문장들과 문장 속 표현들이 7번이나 자연스럽게 반복되는 효과가 있어서 책을 따라 하다 보면 자동적으로 암기가 가능합니다.

★ MP3 파일을 반복해서 들으면 암기에 더욱 효과적입니다.
책에 실린 모든 문장은 초등학생 원어민 성우 Arthur와 Claire가 미국 현지에서 녹음했습니다.

✏ 세이펜으로 더 쉽게, 더 자주 반복해서 들을 수 있습니다.
또한, Study words & chunks의 게임 기능을 통해 더욱 재미있게 암기할 수 있습니다.

4 이해와 기억을 돕는 1,337개의 그림

그림과 상황을 통해 문장의 의미를 직관적으로 이해할 수 있도록 1,001개의 표현을 묘사한 그림과 336개의 대화 상황을 나타내는 그림을 실었습니다.

my mistake

5 또래 원어민 친구와 나눠보는 대화

각 트랙의 마지막 페이지에는 학습한 문장을 채워볼 수 있는 dialogue 4개가 실려 있습니다. 이 대화는 모두 뉴욕에 거주하는 초등학생 원어민 성우 Eden과 Kara가 미국 현지에서 녹음한 것으로, A와 B 중 골라서 role playing을 할 수 있습니다. 꾸준히 연습하다 보면, 실제로 원어민 친구를 만나도 당황하지 않고 자연스럽게 대화할 수 있습니다.

세이펜의 Role-Play 기능을 활용하여 더욱 생생한 대화를 경험해 볼 수 있습니다.
세이펜으로 각 dialogue의 빈칸을 포함한 문장 전체를 녹음한 후 Role-Play 버튼 Ⓡ에 대면,
녹음한 문장이 원어민의 대화와 함께 자연스럽게 재생됩니다.

6 다양한 부가 학습 자료로 완벽 복습

1,001개의 문장을 다양한 부가 학습 자료로 완벽하게 복습할 수 있습니다. 테스트 자료로도 유용하게 활용하실 수 있습니다.
(www.cedubook.com에서 무료로 다운로드 가능합니다.)

어휘리스트 & 어휘테스트
본문에 실린 모든 어휘를 학습할 수 있습니다. 어휘리스트로 학습한 후에는 어휘테스트로 어휘 실력을 점검해볼 수 있습니다.

본문 해석 연습지
1,001개 문장의 해석을 써보며 의미를 복습할 수 있습니다.

본문 말하기·영작 연습지
우리말 해석을 보고 영어로 바꿔 말하거나 써볼 수 있습니다.
말하기·영작 연습지는 '우리말 뜻을 보고 빈칸 채우기 ▶ 순서대로 어휘 배열하기 ▶ 뜻을 보며 영작하기'의 순서로 구성되어 있습니다.

Contents 📖

책속책 **WORKBOOK** | 정답과 해설

Study Plan

★ **20일 완성!**

	Track	공부한 날짜	
1일차	Track 71, 워크북/Track 72, 워크북	월	일
2일차	Track 73, 워크북/Track 74, 워크북	월	일
3일차	Track 71~72 Review	월	일
4일차	Track 73~74 Review	월	일
5일차	Track 75, 워크북/Track 76, 워크북	월	일
6일차	Track 77, 워크북/Track 78, 워크북	월	일
7일차	Track 75~76 Review	월	일
8일차	Track 77~78 Review	월	일
9일차	Track 79, 워크북/Track 80, 워크북	월	일
10일차	Track 81, 워크북/Track 82, 워크북	월	일
11일차	Track 79~80 Review	월	일
12일차	Track 81~82 Review	월	일
13일차	Track 83, 워크북/Track 84, 워크북	월	일
14일차	Track 85, 워크북/Track 86, 워크북	월	일
15일차	Track 83~84 Review	월	일
16일차	Track 85~86 Review	월	일
17일차	Track 87, 워크북/Track 88, 워크북	월	일
18일차	Track 89, 워크북/Track 90, 워크북/Track 91, 워크북	월	일
19일차	Track 87~88 Review	월	일
20일차	Track 89~91 Review	월	일

★ 16일 완성!

	Track	공부한 날짜	
1일차	Track 71~72, 워크북	월	일
2일차	Track 73~74, 워크북	월	일
3일차	Track 75~76, 워크북	월	일
4일차	Track 71~73 Review	월	일
5일차	Track 74~76 Review	월	일
6일차	Track 77~78, 워크북	월	일
7일차	Track 79~80, 워크북	월	일
8일차	Track 81~82, 워크북	월	일
9일차	Track 77~79 Review	월	일
10일차	Track 80~82 Review	월	일
11일차	Track 83~85, 워크북	월	일
12일차	Track 83~85 Review	월	일
13일차	Track 86~88, 워크북	월	일
14일차	Track 86~88 Review	월	일
15일차	Track 89~91, 워크북	월	일
16일차	Track 89~91 Review	월	일

Let's Start!

71
Track

I started feeling sick.

나는 ~하는 것을(~하기) 시작했어.

Say it! 과거에 시작된 나의 행동이나 상태를 말할 때
*started 대신에 began(시작했다)을 써도 같은 뜻이에요.

Fill it! Listen to the track and fill in the blanks with the correct sentence number.

I started -ing.

625 I started feeling sick.

626 I started feeling a little sleepy.

627 I started loving the singer.

628 I started doing my homework.

629 I started reading it last night.

630 I started worrying about the test.

631 I started learning English last year.

632 I started taking after-school classes.

633 I started taking an interest in football.

Study words & chunks!

⭐ Choose the correct words or chunks for each sentence and fill in the blanks. ▷

feeling a little sleepy

learning English

doing my homework

taking after-school classes

loving the singer

feeling sick

taking an interest in football

reading it

worrying about the test

625 I started _____. (아픈 것)

626 I started _____. (조금 졸린 것)

627 I started _____. (그 가수를 정말 좋아하는 것)

628 I started _____. (내 숙제를 하는 것)

629 I started _____ last night. (그것을 읽는 것)

630 I started _____. (시험에 대해 걱정하는 것)

631 I started _____ last year. (영어를 배우는 것)

632 I started _____. (방과 후 수업을 듣는 것)

633 I started _____. (축구에 흥미를 갖는 것)

Guess it!

⭐ In each picture, what would he or she most likely say?
Using 'I **started -ing.**' make a sentence with the words or chunks below.

loving the singer	feeling sick	doing my homework
taking after-school classes	feeling a little sleepy	taking an interest in football
worrying about the test	reading it	learning English

1.
_____
_____ .

Can you speak English? Yes!

2.
_____
_____ last year.

3.
_____
_____ .

Speak Up!

⭐ Complete the dialogues with the best sentence from this track.

> **보기**
>
> **A: I started worrying about the test**.
>
> **B:** Relax. There are only ten questions. It will be okay.

1

A: What's that book about? The book cover looks interesting.

B: I don't know much about it yet. 🎤 _____ ▷

last night.

Ⓡ

2

A: Did you really make this robot?

B: Yes, I made it in class. 🎤 _____

_____ ▷.

A: I want to take that class, too! It looks like so much fun.

Ⓡ

3

A: 🎤 _____ ▷.

B: The class is almost over. Don't fall asleep yet.

Ⓡ

> 세이펜을 통해 각 상황에 맞는 말을 직접 녹음해 보고 확실히 익혔는지 확인해보세요.

📖📖 **[보기]** relax 긴장을 풀다 **1.** book cover 책표지 | look ~해 보이다 | interesting 재미있는 | yet 아직 **2.** really 정말로 | robot 로봇 | make[made] 만들다[만들었다] | want to ~하고 싶다 | like ~처럼 **3.** fall asleep 잠들다

72 Track

I began to get bored.

나는 ~하는 것을(~하기) 시작했어.

Say It! 과거에 시작된 나의 행동이나 상태를 말할 때
*began 대신에 started(시작했다)를 써도 같은 뜻이에요.

Fill it! Listen to the track and fill in the blanks with the correct sentence number.

I began ~.

A.

B.

C.

D.

E.

F.

G.

H.

I.

634 I began to understand.	**639** I began to feel nervous.
635 I began to calm down.	**640** I began to sweat.
636 I began to get upset.	**641** I began to wonder why.
637 I began to get bored.	**642** I began to regret my decision.
638 I began to feel ill.	

Study words & chunks!

⭐ Choose the correct words or chunks for each sentence and fill in the blanks. ▷

to understand

to get bored

to feel ill

to get upset

to calm down

to regret my decision

to sweat

to feel nervous

to wonder why

634 I began _____. (이해하는 것)

635 I began _____. (진정하는 것)

636 I began _____. (화가 나는 것)

637 I began _____. (지루해지는 것)

638 I began _____. (아픈 것)

639 I began _____. (긴장하는 것)

640 I began _____. (땀을 흘리는 것)

641 I began _____. (왜인지 궁금해하는 것)

642 I began _____. (내 결정을 후회하는 것)

Guess it!

⭐ In each picture, what would he or she most likely say?
Using '**I began ~.**' make a sentence with the words or chunks below.

to feel ill	**to feel nervous**	**to understand**
to regret my decision	**to calm down**	**to get upset**
to get bored	**to sweat**	**to wonder why**

1.
_____
_____ .

2.
_____
_____ .

3.
_____
_____ .

Speak Up!

★ Complete the dialogues with the best sentence from this track.

보기

A: How did you do on your listening test?

B: **I began to feel nervous**. So I made a few mistakes.

1

A: I quit piano lessons.

B: Why? You liked it.

A: 🎤 _____ ▷. I'm going to learn something

more fun.

Ⓡ

2

A: Why didn't you come to school yesterday?

B: 🎤 _____ ▷. So I had to stay home.

Ⓡ

3

A: What are you searching for on the Internet?

B: I heard cars can run on coconuts. And 🎤 _____ ▷.

A: So, what did you find?

Ⓡ

세이펜을 통해 각 상황에 맞는 말을 직접 녹음해
보고 확실히 익혔는지 확인해보세요.

📖 **[보기]** make[made] a mistake 실수를 하다[했다] | a few 조금 **1.** quit[quit] 그만두다[그만뒀다] | piano 피아노
| am[are, is] going to ~할 것이다 | more 더 (많이) **2.** have[had] to ~해야 한다[했다] **3.** search for ~을 찾
다 | Internet 인터넷 | hear[heard] 듣다[들었다] | run on ~을 연료로 사용하다 | coconut 코코넛

73 Track

Stop talking about that.

~하는 것을 그만해(그만 ~해).

Say It! 상대방에게 어떤 행동을 그만하라고 말할 때

Fill it! Listen to the track and fill in the blanks with the correct sentence number.

I.

A.

B.

H.

Stop -ing.

C.

G.

F.

E.

D.

643 Stop talking about that.

644 Stop asking me questions.

645 Stop being so picky!

646 Stop making that noise.

647 Stop arguing.

648 Stop complaining!

649 Stop bothering me.

650 Stop fooling around.

651 Stop blaming yourself.

Study words & chunks!

⭐ Choose the correct words or chunks for each sentence and fill in the blanks. ▶

arguing

complaining

being so picky

bothering me

blaming yourself

talking about that

asking me questions

making that noise

fooling around

643 Stop _____. (그것에 대해 이야기하는 것)

644 Stop _____. (나에게 질문들을 하는 것)

645 Stop _____! (까다롭게 구는 것)

646 Stop _____. (시끄럽게 하는 것)

647 Stop _____. (다투는 것)

648 Stop _____! (불평하는 것)

649 Stop _____. (나를 귀찮게 하는 것)

650 Stop _____. (장난치는 것)

651 Stop _____. (너 자신을 탓하는 것)

Guess it!

★ In each picture, what would he or she most likely say?
  Using '**Stop -ing.**' make a sentence with the words or chunks below.

bothering me	making that noise	arguing
fooling around	blaming yourself	being so picky
asking me questions	talking about that	complaining

1.

_____

_____

2.

_____

_____

3.

_____

_____

Speak Up!

⭐ Complete the dialogues with the best sentence from this track.

보기

> A: I will get a ham sandwich. What about you?
>
> B: I don't know. I don't like cucumbers, carrots, and cheese...
>   And I also can't eat...
>
> A: **Stop being so picky**!

1

A: What's the answer? How did you solve it? Was it easy for you?

B: 🎤 _____ ▷. I can't answer all your questions.

A: Sorry. I'll ask one by one.

Ⓡ

2

A: I hate rainy days. My clothes always get wet in the rain. Besides,
   I can't play soccer!

B: 🎤 _____ ▷! It's not going to rain forever.

Ⓡ

3

A: I scored two goals for the other team. Everyone will hate me.

B: They won't. 🎤 _____ ▷. We all make mistakes.

Ⓡ

세이펜을 통해 각 상황에 맞는 말을 직접 녹음해
보고 확실히 익혔는지 확인해보세요.

📖📖 [보기] ham sandwich 햄 샌드위치 | What about ~? ~은 어때? | cucumber 오이 | cheese 치즈 **1.** solve
해결하다, 풀다 | one by one 하나하나씩 **2.** rainy 비가 오는 | get wet 젖다 | besides 게다가 | is[am, are]
going to ~할 것이다 **3.** score[scored] a goal 골을 넣다[넣었다]

I kept standing there.

나[우리]는 ~하는 것을 계속했어(계속 ~했어).

Say it! 내가 예전에 계속했던 일에 대해 말할 때

Fill it! Listen to the track and fill in the blanks with the correct sentence number.

I.

A.

B.

H.

I[We] kept -ing.

C.

G.

F.

E.

D.

652 I kept standing there.

653 I kept waiting for you.

654 I kept making mistakes.

655 We kept playing for hours.

656 We kept practicing soccer.

657 I kept dozing off.

658 I kept yawning all day.

659 I kept thinking about the problem.

660 I kept laughing at his jokes.

Study words & chunks!

⭐ Choose the correct words or chunks for each sentence and fill in the blanks. ▷

waiting for you

playing

making mistakes

practicing soccer

laughing at his jokes

dozing off

yawning

standing there

**thinking about
the problem**

652 I kept _____. (그곳에 서 있는 것)

653 I kept _____. (너를 기다리는 것)

654 I kept _____. (실수들을 하는 것)

655 We kept _____ for hours. (노는 것) * for hours 몇 시간 동안

656 We kept _____. (축구를 연습하는 것)

657 I kept _____. (꾸벅꾸벅 조는 것)

658 I kept _____ all day. (하품하는 것) * all day 온종일

659 I kept _____. (그 문제에 대해 생각하는 것)

660 I kept _____. (그의 농담에 웃는 것)

Guess it!

⭐ In each picture, what would he or she most likely say?
Using '**I[We] kept -ing.**' make a sentence with the words or chunks below.

waiting for you	laughing at his jokes	playing
practicing soccer	yawning	standing there
thinking about the problem	making mistakes	dozing off

1.

_____

_____ all day.

2.

_____

_____.

3.

_____

_____.

Speak Up!

⭐ Complete the dialogues with the best sentence from this track.

> **보기**
>
> A: Did you have fun with them yesterday?
>
> B: Yes. **We kept playing** for hours.
>
> A: Sounds great. I'll join you next time.

1

A: How was the contest? Did you do well?

B: No. 🎤 _____ ▷. I was so nervous!

Ⓡ

2

A: Wake up! We are almost there.

B: Oh, I see. 🎤 _____ ▷.   *I see. 그렇구나.

A: I know you are tired, but wake up! We should get off soon.

Ⓡ

3

A: Did you find the answer?

B: No. 🎤 _____ ▷, but

I still don't know.

Ⓡ

> 세이펜을 통해 각 상황에 맞는 말을 직접 녹음해
> 보고 확실히 익혔는지 확인해보세요.

📖 **[보기]** have fun 재미있게 놀다 | next time 다음번 **1.** How was ~? ~은 어땠어? | nervous 긴장한 **2.** tired 피곤한 | get off (버스, 기차 등에서) 내리다 | soon 곧 **3.** still 아직

75 Track

I want to watch TV.

나는 ~하기를 원해(~하고 싶어).

Say It! 내가 하고 싶은 일을 말할 때

Fill it! Listen to the track and fill in the blanks with the correct sentence number.

I want ~.

A. ___
B. ___
C. ___
D. ___
E. ___
F. ___
G. ___
H. ___
I. ___

661 I want to eat pizza.

662 I want to go home.

663 I want to watch TV.

664 I want to play a game.

665 I want to go out and play.

666 I want to talk to you.

667 I want to get new shoes.

668 I want to know about it.

669 I want to drink something cold.

⭐ Choose the correct words or chunks for each sentence and fill in the blanks. ▶

to talk to you

to get new shoes

to drink something cold

to play a game

to know about it

to eat pizza

to go home

to go out and play

to watch TV

661 I want _____. (피자 먹기)

662 I want _____. (집에 가기)

663 I want _____. (TV 보기)

664 I want _____. (게임 하기)

665 I want _____. (나가서 놀기)

666 I want _____. (너에게 이야기하기)

667 I want _____. (새 신발 갖기)

668 I want _____. (그것에 대해 알기)

669 I want _____. (시원한 것 마시기)

Guess it!

⭐ In each picture, what would he or she most likely say?
Using '**I want ~.**' make a sentence with the words or chunks below.

to watch TV	to play a game	to eat pizza
to know about it	to go out and play	to go home
to drink something cold	to get new shoes	to talk to you

1.

_____

_____ .

2.

_____

_____ .

3.

_____

_____ .

Speak Up!

⭐ Complete the dialogues with the best sentence from this track.

> 보기
>
> **A:** The exam is finally over! Do you have any plans?
>
> **B:** **I want to watch TV**. I need some rest.
>
> **A:** Are there any interesting shows on TV?

1

A: I'm so hungry right now.

B: Me, too. 🎤 _____ ▷. How about you?

A: I like pizza. Let's get some.

Ⓡ

2

A: What do you want for your birthday gift?

B: 🎤 _____ ▷. My shoes are old.

A: Good idea! Tell your parents what you want.

Ⓡ

3

A: It's Saturday today. 🎤 _____ ▷.

B: But it's raining a lot. We can't go out.

A: Alright. Then, let's stay inside and watch TV instead.

Ⓡ

세이펜을 통해 각 상황에 맞는 말을 직접 녹음해 보고 확실히 익혔는지 확인해보세요.

📖 **[보기]** finally 드디어, 마침내 | over 끝이 난 | rest 휴식 | interesting 재미있는 **1.** right now 지금 | How about ~? ～은 어때? | let's ～하자 **2.** old 낡은, 오래된 **3.** Saturday 토요일 | a lot 많이 | then 그러면 | instead 대신에

76 Track

I don't want to go alone.

나는 ~하기를 원하지 않아(~하고 싶지 않아).

Say It! 내가 하고 싶지 않은 일을 말할 때

Fill it! Listen to the track and fill in the blanks with the correct sentence number.

I.

A.

B.

H.

I don't want ~.

C.

G.

F.

E.

D.

---

670 I don't want to go alone.

671 I don't want to study today.

672 I don't want to wake up early.

673 I don't want to answer that.

674 I don't want to bother you.

675 I don't want to eat spinach.

676 I don't want to give up.

677 I don't want to mess up.

678 I don't want to argue with you.

Study words & chunks!

⭐ Choose the correct words or chunks for each sentence and fill in the blanks. ▷

to mess up

to bother you

to wake up early

to eat spinach

to go alone

to argue with you

to study

to answer that

to give up

670 I don't want _____. (혼자 가기)

671 I don't want _____ today. (공부하기)

672 I don't want _____. (일찍 일어나기)

673 I don't want _____. (그것에 대답하기)

674 I don't want _____. (너를 귀찮게 하기)

675 I don't want _____. (시금치를 먹기)

676 I don't want _____. (포기하기)

677 I don't want _____. (망치기)

678 I don't want _____. (너와 말다툼하기)

Guess it!

★ In each picture, what would he or she most likely say?
Using '**I don't want ~.**' make a sentence with the words or chunks below.

to answer that	to study	to eat spinach
to argue with you	to give up	to bother you
to wake up early	to go alone	to mess up

1. _____
_____ .

2. _____
_____ .

3. _____
_____ .

Speak Up!

⭐ Complete the dialogues with the best sentence from this track.

> **A: I don't want to study** today.
>
> **B:** Why?
>
> **A:** It's Saturday. Weekends are for going out and playing!

1

A: Will you come to her birthday party?

B: I am not sure yet.

A: You should come. 🎤 _____ ▷ .

Ⓡ

2

A: What's your phone's password?

B: 🎤 _____ ▷ . It's my secret!

A: Okay. I won't ask you then.

Ⓡ

3

A: You became the captain of your team.

B: Right. I will do my best. 🎤 _____ ▷ .

Ⓡ

세이펜을 통해 각 상황에 맞는 말을 직접 녹음해
보고 확실히 익혔는지 확인해보세요.

📖 **[보기]** Saturday 토요일 **1.** party 파티 | sure 확실한 | yet 아직 **2.** password 비밀번호 | secret 비밀 | then
그러면 **3.** become[became] (무엇이) 되다[되었다] | team 팀, 조 | do my best (내가) 최선을 다하다

Track 77

I wanted to win the game.

나는 ~하기를 원했어(~하고 싶었어).

Say it! 내가 과거에 하고 싶었던 것을 말할 때

Fill it! Listen to the track and fill in the blanks with the correct sentence number.

I wanted ~.

A.

B.

C.

D.

E.

F.

G.

H.

I.

679 I wanted to say sorry.

680 I wanted to look cool.

681 I wanted to buy that.

682 I wanted to win the game.

683 I wanted to go to sleep.

684 I wanted to go to the movies.

685 I wanted to tell you about it.

686 I wanted to ask you something.

687 I wanted to be friends with you.

Study words & chunks!

⭐ Choose the correct words or chunks for each sentence and fill in the blanks. ▷

to ask you something

to go to the movies

to go to sleep

to be friends with you

to look cool

to win the game

to tell you about it

to buy that

to say sorry

679 I wanted _____. (미안하다고 말하기, 사과하기)

680 I wanted _____. (멋있게 보이기)

681 I wanted _____. (저것을 사기)

682 I wanted _____. (경기에서 이기기)

683 I wanted _____. (잠들기)

684 I wanted _____. (영화 보러 가기)

685 I wanted _____. (너에게 그것에 대해 말하기)

686 I wanted _____. (너에게 무언가를 물어보기)

687 I wanted _____. (너와 친해지기, 너와 친구가 되기)

Guess it!

⭐ In each picture, what would he or she most likely say?
Using 'I **wanted** ~.' make a sentence with the words or chunks below.

to ask you something	to go to sleep	to say sorry
to tell you about it	to look cool	to buy that
to be friends with you	to go to the movies	to win the game

1.
_____
_____

2.
_____
_____.

3.
_____
_____.

Speak Up!

⭐ Complete the dialogues with the best sentence from this track.

> **A:** Why are you wearing your cap backwards?
>
> **B:** **I wanted to look cool**.
>
> **A:** But you don't look cool at all! Take it off!

1

A: 🎤 _____ ▷. But we went

shopping instead.

B: Why?

A: My brother had to get new soccer shoes.   Ⓡ

2

A: Did you call me last night?

B: I did. 🎤 _____ ▷.

A: What was it about?   Ⓡ

3

A: A new student will come to our class today.

B: I know. 🎤 _____ ▷, but you left

early yesterday.   *I know. 맞아.   Ⓡ

세이펜을 통해 각 상황에 맞는 말을 직접 녹음해
보고 확실히 익혔는지 확인해보세요.

📖 **[보기]** backwards 거꾸로 | not ~ at all 결코 ~하지 않는 | take off ~을 벗다 **1.** go[went] shopping 쇼핑하러
가다[갔다] | instead 대신에 | have[had] to ~해야 한다[했다] **3.** leave[left] 떠나다[떠났다]

78 Track

I like to travel.

나는 ~하는 것을 좋아해.

Say it! 내가 좋아하는 활동을 말할 때
*매우 좋아하는 것을 말할 때는 like 대신에 love를 쓰기도 해요.

Fill it! Listen to the track and fill in the blanks with the correct sentence number.

I like ~.

H.   I.   A.   B.   C.   G.   F.   E.   D.

688 I like to travel.

689 I like to stay home.

690 I like to play sports.

691 I like to take pictures.

692 I like to watch TV shows.

693 I like to hear scary stories.

694 I like to learn new things.

695 I like to talk with my friends.

696 I like to hang out with my friends.

Study words & chunks!

⭐ Choose the correct words or chunks for each sentence and fill in the blanks. ▷

to hear scary stories

to talk with my friends

to travel

to hang out with
my friends

to learn new things

to take pictures

to stay home

to watch TV shows

to play sports

688 I like _____. (여행하는 것)

689 I like _____. (집에 머무는 것)

690 I like _____. (운동하는 것)

691 I like _____. (사진 찍는 것)

692 I like _____. (TV 쇼 보는 것)

693 I like _____. (무서운 이야기를 듣는 것)

694 I like _____. (새로운 것들을 배우는 것)

695 I like _____. (내 친구들과 이야기하는 것)

696 I like _____. (내 친구들과 시간을 보내는 것)

Guess it!

⭐ In each picture, what would he or she most likely say?
Using '**I like ~.**' make a sentence with the words or chunks below.

to play sports	to hang out with my friends	to stay home
to travel	to watch TV shows	to learn new things
to hear scary stories	to talk with my friends	to take pictures

1. _____
_____ .

2. _____
_____ .

3. _____
_____ .

Speak Up!

⭐ Complete the dialogues with the best sentence from this track.

보기

A: I started to learn Chinese yesterday.

B: You are also learning to swim. Aren't you getting tired?

A: Not at all. I enjoy learning. **I like to learn new things**.

*Not at all. 전혀 그렇지 않아.

1

A: You know what? I saw a ghost!　　　　*You know what? 너 그거 알아?

B: Really? Tell me more about it! 🎤 _____

_____ ▷.

Ⓡ

2

A: What do you like to do at home?

B: 🎤 _____ ▷.

A: Me, too. I love all the weekend TV shows.

Ⓡ

3

A: What do you do after school?

B: 🎤 _____ ▷. I usually play soccer

or basketball with my friends.

A: Me, too. I especially like baseball.

Ⓡ

세이펜을 통해 각 상황에 맞는 말을 직접 녹음해
보고 확실히 익혔는지 확인해보세요.

📖 **[보기]** Chinese 중국어 | learn to ~하는 것을 배우다 | get tired 피곤해지다 **1.** see[saw] 보다[보았다] | really
정말 | more 더 (많이) **3.** usually 보통 | especially 특히

I need to talk to you.

나는 ~하는 것이 필요해(~해야 해).

Say It! 내가 해야 하는 행동을 말할 때

Fill it! Listen to the track and fill in the blanks with the correct sentence number.

I. | A. | B. | H. | **I need ~.** | C. | G. | F. | E. | D.

---

697 I need to hurry.

698 I need to talk to you.

699 I need to call my mom.

700 I need to go to the bathroom.

701 I need to wash my hands.

702 I need to stay calm.

703 I need to get a good grade.

704 I need to get ready for school.

705 I need to ask you a question.

Study words & chunks!

⭐ Choose the correct words or chunks for each sentence and fill in the blanks. ▷

to talk to you

to ask you a question

to call my mom

to go to the bathroom

to stay calm

to get ready for school

to wash my hands

to get a good grade

to hurry

697 I need _____. (서두르는 것)

698 I need _____. (너에게 이야기하는 것)

699 I need _____. (엄마께 전화하는 것)

700 I need _____. (화장실 가는 것)

701 I need _____. (내 손을 씻는 것)

702 I need _____. (침착하는 것)

703 I need _____. (좋은 성적을 받는 것)

704 I need _____. (학교 갈 준비를 하는 것)

705 I need _____. (너에게 질문하는 것)

Guess it!

⭐ In each picture, what would he or she most likely say?
Using '**I need ~.**' make a sentence with the words or chunks below.

to ask you a question	to call my mom	to stay calm
to get ready for school	to hurry	to talk to you
to go to the bathroom	to wash my hands	to get a good grade

1.

_____

_____ .

2.

_____

_____ .

3.

_____

_____ .

Speak Up!

⭐ Complete the dialogues with the best sentence from this track.

보기

> **A:** It's already six o'clock! Why don't you have dinner at my house?
>
> **B:** I don't know. **I need to call my mom**. She is waiting for me.

1

A: 🎤 _____ ▷.

B: Why? You always do.

A: I'll get a perfect score this time. Then, my dad will buy me a bike.

Ⓡ

2

A: What's the matter? You look so sick.

B: Oh... my stomach is killing me. 🎤 _____

_____ ▷.

A: You should. The bathroom is right over there.

Ⓡ

3

A: Our teacher will pick the winner soon.

B: I know. 🎤 _____ ▷, but I am so nervous!

I really want to be the winner.   *I know. 맞아.

A: Don't be nervous. I am sure you will win!

Ⓡ

> 세이펜을 통해 각 상황에 맞는 말을 직접 녹음해
> 보고 확실히 익혔는지 확인해보세요.

📖 **[보기]** Why don't you ~? 너는 ~하는 게 어때? **1.** perfect score 만점 | this time 이번 | then 그러면 **2.** stomach 배 | kill ~에게 심한 고통을 주다 | right 바로 | over there 저쪽에 **3.** pick 뽑다, 고르다 | winner 우승자 | soon 곧 | nervous 긴장한

80
Track

I tried to call you.

나는 ~하려고 (노력)했어.

Say It! 내가 과거에 하려고 했던 일이나 하려고 노력했던 일에 대해 말할 때

Fill it! Listen to the track and fill in the blanks with the correct sentence number.

I tried ~.

H.

I.

A.

B.

C.

G.

F.

E.

D.

706 I tried to be nice.	**711** I tried to cheer up my friend.
707 I tried to call you.	**712** I tried to fall asleep.
708 I tried to do my best.	**713** I tried to be patient.
709 I tried to finish my homework.	**714** I tried to play less computer games.
710 I tried to solve the problem.	

Study words & chunks!

⭐ Choose the correct words or chunks for each sentence and fill in the blanks. ▷

to cheer up my friend

to fall asleep

to solve the problem

to do my best

to be nice

to be patient

to call you

to play less
computer games

to finish my homework

706 I tried _____ . (친절한 것)

707 I tried _____ . (너에게 전화하는 것)

708 I tried _____ . (내가 최선을 다하는 것)

709 I tried _____ . (내 숙제를 끝내는 것)

710 I tried _____ . (문제를 해결하는 것)

711 I tried _____ . (내 친구를 격려하는 것)

712 I tried _____ . (잠드는 것)

713 I tried _____ . (참을성 있는 것)

714 I tried _____ . (컴퓨터 게임을 덜 하는 것)

Guess it!

⭐ In each picture, what would he or she most likely say?
Using '**I tried ~.**' make a sentence with the words or chunks below.

to be patient	to fall asleep	to call you
to finish my homework	to cheer up my friend	to solve the problem
to play less computer games	to do my best	to be nice

1. _____ .

2. _____ .

3. _____ .

Speak Up!

⭐ Complete the dialogues with the best sentence from this track.

> 보기
>
> **A: I tried to cheer up my friend.**
>
> B: What happened to him?
>
> A: He broke his leg while riding a bicycle. He is in the hospital now.

1

A: Why are you mean to him?

B: 🎤 _____ ▷, but he made fun of me.

A: Maybe he just wants to be friends with you.

Ⓡ

2

A: 🎤 _____ ▷, but I am so hungry! I can't wait any longer.

B: Relax. It's almost our turn. We will get our lunch soon.

Ⓡ

3

A: You didn't show up yesterday. What happened?

B: 🎤 _____ ▷. But I lost my cell phone.

Ⓡ

세이펜을 통해 각 상황에 맞는 맞은 직접 녹음해 보고 확실히 익혔는지 확인해보세요.

📖 **[보기]** break[broke] 부러지다[부러졌다] | while ~하는 동안 | ride (자전거를) 타다 **1.** mean 심술궂은 | make[made] fun of ~를 놀리다[놀렸다] | maybe 아마도 **2.** any longer 더 이상 | relax 진정하다 | turn 차례 | soon 곧 **3.** show up (예정된 장소에) 나타나다, 나오다 | lose[lost] 잃어버리다[잃어버렸다] | cell phone 휴대폰

정답과 해설 p.9

81 Track

I'm supposed to clean my room.

나는 ~하기로 되어 있어(~해야 해).

Say It! 내가 할 예정이거나 해야 하는 일을 말할 때

Fill it! Listen to the track and fill in the blanks with the correct sentence number.

I.

A.

B.

H.

I'm supposed to ~.

C.

G.

F.

E.

D.

- **715** I'm supposed to help my mom.
- **716** I'm supposed to meet my friends.
- **717** I'm supposed to clean my room.
- **718** I'm supposed to be home right now!
- **719** I'm supposed to be in class by nine.
- **720** I'm supposed to go to bed by ten.
- **721** I'm supposed to follow the rules.
- **722** I'm supposed to take care of my sister.
- **723** I'm supposed to be in charge.

Study words & chunks!

⭐ Choose the correct words or chunks for each sentence and fill in the blanks. ▷

be home

meet my friends

be in charge

follow the rules

go to bed

clean my room

help my mom

take care of my sister

be in class

715 I'm supposed to _____. (엄마를 돕다)

716 I'm supposed to _____. (내 친구들을 만나다)

717 I'm supposed to _____. (내 방을 청소하다)

718 I'm supposed to _____ right now! (집에 있다) * right now 지금

719 I'm supposed to _____ by nine. (교실에 있다) * by (시간) ~까지

720 I'm supposed to _____ by ten. (잠자리에 들다)

721 I'm supposed to _____. (규칙들을 따르다)

722 I'm supposed to _____. (내 여동생을 돌보다)

723 I'm supposed to _____. (책임을 맡다)

Guess it!

⭐ In each picture, what would he or she most likely say?
Using '**I'm supposed to ~.**' make a sentence with the words or chunks below.

help my mom	be home	go to bed
be in charge	follow the rules	meet my friends.
be in class	clean my room	take care of my sister

1.

_____

_____ by nine.

2.

_____

_____.

3.

_____

_____.

Speak Up!

⭐ Complete the dialogues with the best sentence from this track.

> A: **I'm supposed to take care of my sister**.
>
> B: How do you take care of her?
>
> A: I walk her to her classroom every morning.

1

A: Do you have any plans today?

B: 🎤 _____ ▷.

We are going to see a movie.

Ⓡ

2

A: Where are you going?

B: 🎤 _____ ▷. It's a mess.

A: My mom complains about my messy room, too.

Ⓡ

3

A: What time do you go to sleep?

B: 🎤 _____ ▷ by ten. But I want to

stay up late tonight.

Ⓡ

세이펜을 통해 각 상황에 맞는 말을 직접 녹음해
보고 확실히 익혔는지 확인해보세요.

📖 [보기] walk (걸어서) 바래다주다 **1.** are[am, is] going to ~할 것이다 **2.** mess 엉망진창 | complain about ~에 대해 불평하다 | messy 지저분한 **3.** go to sleep 잠들다 | stay up late 늦게까지 깨어있다[자지 않고 있다]

82 Track

It's time to get ready.

~할 시간이야.

Say It! 무엇을 할 시간인지 말할 때

Fill it! Listen to the track and fill in the blanks with the correct sentence number.

I.

A.

B.

H.

It's time to ~.

C.

G.

F.

E.

D.

724 It's time to wake up.

725 It's time to get ready.

726 It's time to leave.

727 It's time to have fun!

728 It's time to clean our classroom.

729 It's time to go to the music room.

730 It's time to get on the shuttle bus.

731 It's time to wrap up.

732 It's time to make a decision.

Study words & chunks!

⭐ Choose the correct words or chunks for each sentence and fill in the blanks. ▷

get on the shuttle bus

wake up

clean our classroom

leave

wrap up

have fun

make a decision

go to the music room

get ready

724 It's time to _____. (일어나다)

725 It's time to _____. (준비하다)

726 It's time to _____. (떠나다)

727 It's time to _____! (재미있게 놀다)

728 It's time to _____. (우리 교실을 청소하다)

729 It's time to _____. (음악실에 가다)

730 It's time to _____. (셔틀버스에 타다)

731 It's time to _____. (끝내다)

732 It's time to _____. (결정하다)

Guess it!

⭐ In each picture, what would he or she most likely say?
Using 'It's time to ~.' make a sentence with the words or chunks below.

wake up	go to the music room	leave
have fun	wrap up	get ready
make a decision	clean our classroom	get on the shuttle bus

1.

_____

_____ .

2.

_____

_____ .

3.

_____

_____ .

Speak Up!

⭐ Complete the dialogues with the best sentence from this track.

A: It's time to wrap up.

B: Already? But I'm not finished yet. Give me more time.

A: I can't. Our teacher is waiting.

1

A: 🎙 _____ ▷.

B: Great! I love music class. Let's go.

A: Wait. Don't forget to take your textbook with you!

Ⓡ

2

A: I'm nervous about the race! It's our turn soon.

B: Yes, 🎙 _____ ▷. Don't be nervous. We can win this race!

Ⓡ

3

A: 🎙 _____ ▷!

B: Yes. We finally finished our group homework.

A: Yay! Now we can play!

*Yay! 야호!

Ⓡ

세이펜을 통해 각 상황에 맞는 말을 직접 녹음해 보고 확실히 익혔는지 확인해보세요.

📖 [보기] finished 끝난 | yet 아직 | more 더 (많은) **1.** let's ~하자 **2.** nervous 긴장한 | turn 차례 | soon 곧
3. finally 드디어

83 Track

Do you know how to do it?

너는 ~하는 법을(~할 줄) 알아?

Say It! 상대방에게 어떤 행동을 하는 방법을 아는지 물어볼 때

Fill it! Listen to the track and fill in the blanks with the correct sentence number.

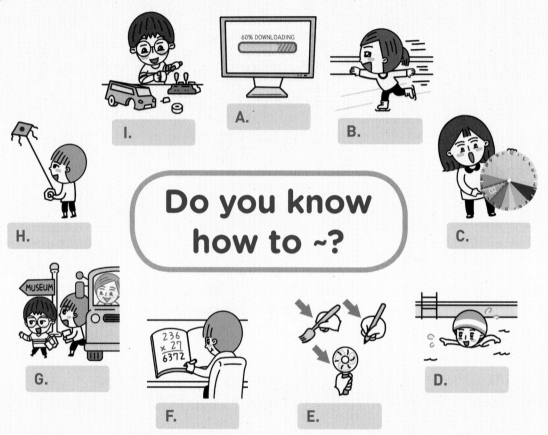

I.　A.　B.

H.

Do you know how to ~?

C.

G.　F.　E.　D.

733 Do you know how to swim?

734 Do you know how to do it?

735 Do you know how to use it?

736 Do you know how to fix it?

737 Do you know how to skate?

738 Do you know how to fly a kite?

739 Do you know how to get there?

740 Do you know how to download it?

741 Do you know how to solve the problem?

Study words & chunks!

⭐ Choose the correct words or chunks for each sentence and fill in the blanks. ▷

skate

download it

do it

swim

get there

fix it

solve the problem

use it

fly a kite

733 Do you know how to _____? (수영하다)

734 Do you know how to _____? (그것을 하다)

735 Do you know how to _____? (그것을 사용하다)

736 Do you know how to _____? (그것을 고치다)

737 Do you know how to _____? (스케이트를 타다)

738 Do you know how to _____? (연을 날리다)

739 Do you know how to _____? (그곳에 도착하다, 그곳에 가다)

740 Do you know how to _____? (그것을 다운로드하다)

741 Do you know how to _____? (그 문제를 풀다)

Guess it!

★ In each picture, what would he or she most likely say?
Using '**Do you know how to ~?**' make a sentence with the words or chunks below.

solve the problem	use it	swim
fly a kite	do it	download it
skate	fix it	get there

1.

_____

_____ ?

2.

_____

_____ ?

3.

_____

_____ ?

Speak Up!

⭐ Complete the dialogues with the best sentence from this track.

> **보기**
>
> **A:** This is my mother's new coffee maker.
>
> **B: Do you know how to use it**?
>
> **A:** Of course not. I don't drink coffee. Only my mother knows how.
>
> *Of course not. 물론 아니지.

1

A: I can't beat this level. 🎤 _____ ▶ ?

B: First, you need a lot of gold. Then you have to buy a new item.

Ⓡ

2

A: Your toy helicopter is broken. 🎤 _____

_____ ▶ ?

B: No, but my dad does. I'll ask him tonight.

Ⓡ

3

A: I went to the new library with my sister yesterday.

B: 🎤 _____ ▶ ?

A: Take bus number 7. You have to go three stops from here.

Ⓡ

> 세이펜을 통해 각 상황에 맞는 말을 직접 녹음해
> 보고 확실히 익혔는지 확인해보세요.

📖 **[보기]** coffee maker 커피 끓이는 기구, 커피 메이커 **1.** beat (게임에서) 이기다 | level 단계, 레벨 | a lot of 많은 | have to ~해야 한다 | item (게임 등의) 아이템 **2.** broken 고장 난 **3.** go[went] 가다[갔다] | take (버스 등을) 타다 | stop 정류장

84 Track

I don't know what to say.

나는 무엇을 ~해야 할지 모르겠어.

Say It! 내가 어떤 행동을 해야 할지 모르겠다고 말할 때

Fill it! Listen to the track and fill in the blanks with the correct sentence number.

I.

A.

B.

I don't know what to ~.

H.

C.

G.

F.

E.

D.

742 I don't know what to do next.

743 I don't know what to say.

744 I don't know what to wear.

745 I don't know what to believe.

746 I don't know what to pick.

747 I don't know what to tell him.

748 I don't know what to order.

749 I don't know what to write about.

750 I don't know what to get her as a gift.

Study words & chunks!

⭐ Choose the correct words or chunks for each sentence and fill in the blanks. ▷

write about

order

say

wear

do

get her as a gift

pick

believe

tell him

742 I don't know what to _____ next. (하다)

743 I don't know what to _____. (말하다)

744 I don't know what to _____. (입다)

745 I don't know what to _____. (믿다)

746 I don't know what to _____. (고르다)

747 I don't know what to _____. (그에게 말하다)

748 I don't know what to _____. (주문하다)

749 I don't know what to _____. (~에 대해 쓰다)

750 I don't know what to _____. (그녀에게 선물로 ~을 주다)

Guess it!

In each picture, what would he or she most likely say?
Using '**I don't know what to ~.**' make a sentence with the words or chunks below.

order	pick	do
believe	write about	tell him
get her as a gift	say	wear

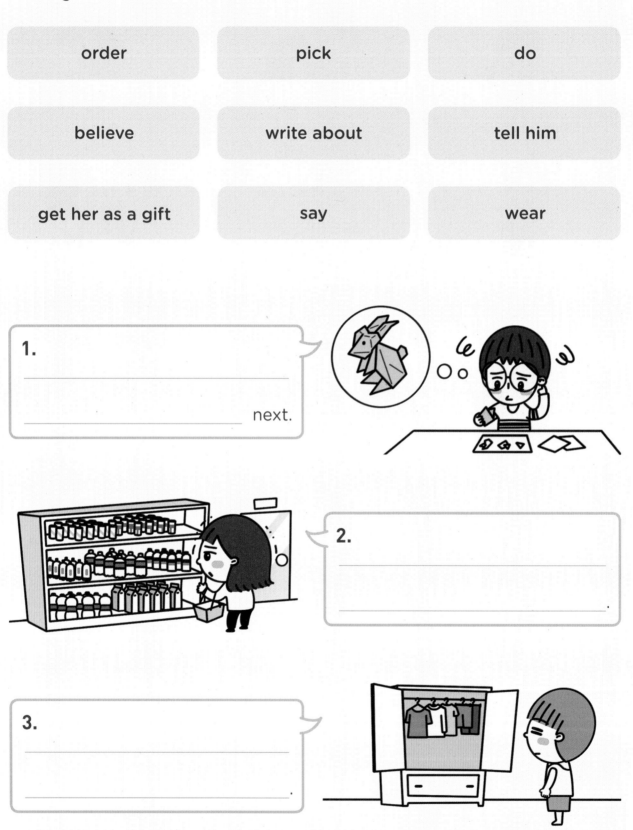

1.

_____

_____ next.

2.

_____

_____.

3.

_____

_____.

Speak Up!

⭐ Complete the dialogues with the best sentence from this track.

> **보기**
>
> **A:** I messed up his work. **I don't know what to tell him**.
>
> **B:** You should explain and say sorry to him. He will understand you.

1

A: My mom's birthday is tomorrow. 🎤 _____

_____ ▷ .

B: How about giving her favorite flowers? My mom loves flowers.

A: That's a great idea.

Ⓡ

2

A: 🎤 _____ ▷ . There are so many

items on the menu.

B: Choose quickly. People are waiting in line.

A: Okay. I just need a few more seconds.

Ⓡ

3

A: Did you start writing?

B: Not yet. 🎤 _____ ▷ .

A: How about writing about your favorite things?

Ⓡ

> 세이펜을 통해 각 상황에 맞는 말을 직접 녹음해
> 보고 확실히 익혔는지 확인해보세요.

📖📖 **[보기]** mess[messed] up ~을 망치다[망쳤다] | work 작품 | explain 설명하다 **1.** How about -ing? ~하는 게
어때? **2.** there are ~이 있다 | item 항목 | menu 메뉴 | quickly 빨리 | wait in line 줄을 서서 기다리다 |
a few more seconds 몇 초만 더 **3.** yet 아직

85 Track

He seems to be busy.

그[그녀]는 ~하는 것처럼 보여(~하는 것 같아).

Say it! 다른 사람의 기분이나 행동이 어때 보이는지 말할 때

Fill it! Listen to the track and fill in the blanks with the correct sentence number.

I.

A.

B.

H.

He[She] seems ~.

C.

G.

F.

E.

D.

---

751 He seems to be busy.

752 She seems to be smart.

753 She seems to be so nice.

754 She seems to be so popular.

755 She seems to need help.

756 He seems to care about you.

757 She seems to have a boyfriend.

758 He seems to be in a bad mood.

759 He seems to be having fun.

Study words & chunks!

⭐ Choose the correct words or chunks for each sentence and fill in the blanks. ▷

to need help

to be so popular

to be busy

to be in a bad mood

to care about you

to be having fun

to be so nice

to have a boyfriend

to be smart

751	He seems	(바쁜 것)
752	She seems	(똑똑한 것)
753	She seems	(정말 착한 것)
754	She seems	(정말 인기가 많은 것)
755	She seems	(도움이 필요한 것)
756	He seems	(너에게 관심을 가지는 것)
757	She seems	(남자친구가 있는 것)
758	He seems	(기분이 나쁜[안 좋은] 것)
759	He seems	(재미있게 놀고 있는 것)

Guess it!

⭐ In each picture, what would he or she most likely say?
Using 'He[She] seems ~.' make a sentence with the words or chunks below.

to be in a bad mood	to care about you	to be having fun
to be so nice	to be smart	to have a boyfriend
to be busy	to need help	to be so popular

1. _____
_____

2. _____
_____

3. _____
_____

Speak Up!

⭐ Complete the dialogues with the best sentence from this track.

보기

> **A:** There he is! Talk to him now.
>
> **B:** I'm not sure. **He seems to be busy**.
>
> **A:** No, I don't think so. He is just packing his bag.

1

A: 🎤 _____ ▷.

B: I know. He didn't even say hi to me this morning.   *I know. 맞아.

A: What's wrong with him?

Ⓡ

2

A: 🎤 _____ ▷. She looks hurt.

B: Are you sure? She is just sitting there.

A: Don't you see the wound on her knee?

Ⓡ

3

A: 🎤 _____ ▷. Maybe he likes you!

B: No way! He just sometimes helps me. That's all.   *No way! 절대 아니야!

A: But he never helps anyone like that.

Ⓡ

> 세이펜을 통해 각 상황에 맞는 말을 직접 녹음해
> 보고 확실히 익혔는지 확인해보세요.

📖 **[보기]** sure 확신하는 | pack (짐을) 싸다 **1.** even 심지어 | say hi 인사하다 | this morning 오늘 아침 **2.** look
~해 보이다 | hurt 다친 | wound 상처 | knee 무릎 **3.** anyone 아무도 | like that 그런 식으로, 그렇게

You look tired.

너는 ~해 보여.

Say It! 상대방의 기분이나 상태가 어때 보이는지 말할 때

Fill it! Listen to the track and fill in the blanks with the correct sentence number.

I.

A.

B.

H.

You look ~.

C.

G.

F.

E.

D.

760 You look happy.	**765** You look excited.
761 You look great.	**766** You look worried.
762 You look angry.	**767** You look surprised.
763 You look tired.	**768** You look confused.
764 You look bored.	

Study words & chunks!

⭐ Choose the correct words or chunks for each sentence and fill in the blanks. ▷

happy

surprised

worried

tired

confused

great

bored

angry

excited

760   You look _____. (행복한)

761   You look _____. (멋진)

762   You look _____. (화난)

763   You look _____. (피곤한)

764   You look _____. (지루해하는)

765   You look _____. (신이 난)

766   You look _____. (걱정스러운)

767   You look _____. (놀란)

768   You look _____. (혼란스러운, 헷갈리는)

Guess it!

⭐ In each picture, what would he or she most likely say?
Using '**You look ~.**' make a sentence with the words or chunks below.

angry	excited	bored
tired	great	worried
surprised	happy	confused

1.

_____

_____ .

What's up?

2.

_____

_____ .

3.

_____

_____ .

Speak Up!

⭐ Complete the dialogues with the best sentence from this track.

> **보기**
>
> **A: You look bored**. What are you reading?
>
> **B:** It's a history book. It's making me sleepy.
>
> **A:** Then, let's do something more fun instead!

1

A: 🎤 _____ ▷. That sweater is the perfect color

for you. Is it new?

B: Yes. My grandma bought it for me.

Ⓡ

2

A: 🎤 _____ ▷. What's wrong?

B: I lost my mom's ring. I can't find it.

A: Oh my! Let me help you find it.   *Oh my! 저런!

Ⓡ

3

A: 🎤 _____ ▷. What happened?

B: Someone stole my pencil case. I need to find out who.

Ⓡ

세이펜을 통해 각 상황에 맞는 말을 직접 녹음해
보고 확실히 익혔는지 확인해보세요.

📖 **[보기]** sleepy 졸린 | something 무엇 | more 더 (많이) | instead 대신에 **1.** sweater 스웨터 | perfect 완벽한
| buy[bought] 사 주다[사 주었다] **2.** lose[lost] 잃어버리다[잃어버렸다] **3.** someone 누군가 | steal[stole] 훔치
다[훔쳤다] | pencil case 필통 | need to ~해야 한다 | find out 알아내다

87
Track

I feel better.

나는 ~한 느낌이야(기분이야).

Say it! 나의 상태나 기분이 어떤지 말할 때
*"I feel sad."는 "I am sad."보다 슬픈 기분을 '느끼는' 것을 더 잘 표현해요.

Fill it! Listen to the track and fill in the blanks with the correct sentence number.

I feel ~.

A.
B.
C.
D.
E.
F.
G.
H.
I.

769 I feel sad.

770 I feel sick.

771 I feel chilly.

772 I feel better.

773 I feel proud.

774 I feel scared.

775 I feel nervous.

776 I feel comfortable.

777 I feel embarrassed.

Study words & chunks!

⭐ Choose the correct words or chunks for each sentence and fill in the blanks. ▷

proud

nervous

chilly

sad

sick

embarrassed

comfortable

scared

better

769 I feel _____ . (슬픈)

770 I feel _____ . (아픈)

771 I feel _____ . (추운, 쌀쌀한)

772 I feel _____ . (몸이 나아진, 기분이 나아진)

773 I feel _____ . (자랑스러운)

774 I feel _____ . (무서운)

775 I feel _____ . (긴장한)

776 I feel _____ . (편안한)

777 I feel _____ . (창피한)

Guess it!

⭐ In each picture, what would he or she most likely say?
Using 'I feel ~.' make a sentence with the words or chunks below.

scared	proud	sad
chilly	embarrassed	better
comfortable	sick	nervous

1.

_____

_____

2.

_____

_____

3.

_____

_____

Speak Up!

⭐ Complete the dialogues with the best sentence from this track.

> **보기**
>
> **A:** Are you okay?
>
> **B:** <u>**I feel nervous**</u>. What if I make a mistake?
>
> **A:** Don't worry about it. No one will notice.

1

A: Let's go out and play. I'm bored.

B: I think I can't. 🎤 _____ ▷. Let's just stay here.

Ⓡ

2

A: How do you feel today? You had a cold yesterday.

B: 🎤 _____ ▷. I took some medicine yesterday.

Ⓡ

3

A: Look at that ghost! 🎤 _____ ▷.

B: Don't worry. It's just a movie.

Ⓡ

세이펜을 통해 각 상황에 맞는 말을 직접 녹음해 보고 확실히 익혔는지 확인해보세요.

📖 **[보기]** What if ~? ~면 어쩌지? | make a mistake 실수하다 | no one 아무도 ~ 않다 | notice 알아채다
1. bored 지루한 **2.** have[had] a cold 감기에 걸리다[걸렸다] | take[took] some medicine 약을 먹다[먹었다]

I got hungry.

나는 ~됐어.

Say it! 내 기분이나 상태가 어떻게 되었는지 말할 때

Fill it! Listen to the track and fill in the blanks with the correct sentence number.

I got ~.

I. A. B. H. C. G. F. E. D.

778 I got hungry.

779 I got mad.

780 I got all wet.

781 I got lucky.

782 I got nervous.

783 I got hurt.

784 I got dizzy.

785 I got carsick.

786 I got sunburned.

Study words & chunks!

⭐ Choose the correct words or chunks for each sentence and fill in the blanks. ▷

all wet

sunburned

dizzy

hurt

hungry

carsick

mad

lucky

nervous

778 I got _____ . (배고픈)

779 I got _____ . (몹시 화가 난)

780 I got _____ . (다 젖은)

781 I got _____ . (운이 좋은)

782 I got _____ . (긴장한)

783 I got _____ . (다친)

784 I got _____ . (어지러운)

785 I got _____ . (차멀미를 하는)

786 I got _____ . (햇볕에 심하게 탄)

Guess it!

⭐ In each picture, what would he or she most likely say?
Using 'I got ~.' make a sentence with the words or chunks below.

carsick	lucky	hungry
dizzy	sunburned	hurt
nervous	mad	all wet

1.
_____
_____ .

2.
_____
_____ .

3.
_____
_____ .

Speak Up!

⭐ Complete the dialogues with the best sentence from this track.

> **보기**
>
> **A:** Why did you eat all the chips?
>
> **B:** I'm sorry. **I got hungry**.
>
> **A:** I was saving those for later!

1

A: What happened to your clothes?

B: The wind turned my umbrella inside out. 🎤_____ ▷.   Ⓡ

2

A: Did you set a new record again in this game?

B: Yes, 🎤_____ ▷. Do you want to play more?

A: No, not really. I will stop here.   *No, not really. 아니, 별로.   Ⓡ

3

A: Why did you cry in the hospital?

B: 🎤_____ ▷. I'm scared of shots.   Ⓡ

> 세이펜을 통해 각 상황에 맞는 말을 직접 녹음해 보고 확실히 익혔는지 확인해보세요.

📖 **[보기]** chip 감자 칩 | save 남겨두다, 아끼다 | later 나중에 **1.** happen[happened] (일이) 일어나다[일어났다] | turn ~ inside out ~을 뒤집다 **2.** set a new record 신기록을 세우다 | want to ~하고 싶다 | more 더 (많이) **3.** scared of ~이 무서운 | shot 주사

89 Track

I'm getting bored.

나는 점점 ~해지고 있어.

Say It! 내 기분이나 상태가 어떻게 되어가고 있는지 말할 때

Fill it! Listen to the track and fill in the blanks with the correct sentence number.

I'm getting ~.

787 I'm getting hungry.		**792** I'm getting nervous.
788 I'm getting full.		**793** I'm getting confused.
789 I'm getting cold.		**794** I'm getting better at it.
790 I'm getting taller.		**795** I'm getting tired of waiting.
791 I'm getting bored.		

Study words & chunks!

 ON OFF

⭐ Choose the correct words or chunks for each sentence and fill in the blanks. ▷

taller

bored

nervous

tired of waiting

full

hungry

better at it

cold

confused

787 I'm getting _____. (배고픈)

788 I'm getting _____. (배부른)

789 I'm getting _____. (추운)

790 I'm getting _____. (키가 더 큰)

791 I'm getting _____. (지루한)

792 I'm getting _____. (긴장한)

793 I'm getting _____. (혼란스러운, 헷갈리는)

794 I'm getting _____. (그것을 더 잘하는)

795 I'm getting _____. (기다리는 것에 지친)

Guess it!

⭐ In each picture, what would he or she most likely say?
Using '**I'm getting ~.**' make a sentence with the words or chunks below.

cold	taller	hungry
full	tired of waiting	better at it
nervous	bored	confused

1.
_____
_____ .

2.
_____
_____ .

3.
_____
_____ .

Speak Up!

⭐ Complete the dialogues with the best sentence from this track.

> **보기**
>
> **A:** The line is really long for this ride.
>
> **B:** When is our turn coming? **I'm getting tired of waiting**.
>
> **A:** We have to wait for another half an hour.

1

A: Which bus do we have to take? Number 10 or 11?

B: I think the number 10 bus... Wait. 🎤 _____ ▷.

A: Let's check the bus route map over there. Ⓡ

2

A: Are you still going swimming after school these days?

B: Yes. 🎤 _____ ▷. I want to swim in the sea this summer.

A: That sounds awesome. Ⓡ

3

A: 🎤 _____ ▷. This baseball game is so boring!

B: Already? But the game just started!

A: I'm not a big fan of baseball. Can we watch something else? Ⓡ

> 세이펜을 통해 각 상황에 맞는 말을 직접 녹음해 보고 확실히 익혔는지 확인해보세요.

📖 **[보기]** really 정말로 | ride 놀이기구 | turn 차례 | have to ~해야 한다 | half an hour 30분 **1.** which 어느, 어떤 | take (버스 등을) 타다 | let's ~하자 | bus route map 버스 노선도 | over there 저쪽에 **2.** still 여전히 | these days 요즘에는 | awesome 아주 멋진 **3.** boring 지루한 | something else 다른 것

90
Track

She seems so busy.

그[그녀]는 ~인 것처럼 보여(~인 것 같아).

Say It! 다른 사람의 모습이나 상태가 어때 보이는지 말할 때

Fill it! Listen to the track and fill in the blanks with the correct sentence number.

I.

A.

B.

H.

He[She] seems ~.

C.

G.

F.

E.

D.

---

796 He seems sick.

797 She seems smart.

798 She seems so busy.

799 She seems so sure.

800 He seems different today.

801 He seems friendly.

802 He seems strange.

803 She seems strict.

804 He seems interested in you.

ON OFF

⭐ Choose the correct words or chunks for each sentence and fill in the blanks. ▷

strange

different

interested in you

strict

smart

sick

so busy

so sure

friendly

796	He seems _____.	(아픈)
797	She seems _____.	(똑똑한)
798	She seems _____.	(매우 바쁜)
799	She seems _____.	(매우 확신하는)
800	He seems _____ today.	(다른)
801	He seems _____.	(친절한)
802	He seems _____.	(이상한)
803	She seems _____.	(엄격한)
804	He seems _____.	(너에게 관심이 있는)

Guess it!

⭐ In each picture, what would he or she most likely say?
    Using '**He[She] seems ~.**' make a sentence with the words or chunks below.

so sure	smart	interested in you
so busy	strict	sick
friendly	different	strange

1.
_____

2.
_____

3.
_____

Speak Up!

⭐ Complete the dialogues with the best sentence from this track.

> **보기**
>
> **A:** <u>**He seems interested in you**</u>. Maybe he likes you.
>
> **B:** Why do you say that?
>
> **A:** He keeps looking at you in class. And he acts so nice only to you.

1

A: 🎤 _____ ▷ today.

B: Yes, he does. Did he get a haircut?

A: I guess so.
*I guess so. 그런 것 같아. ⓡ

2

A: Let's take a picture here!

B: Okay! We can ask someone to take a picture of us.

A: Let's ask that person. 🎤 _____ ▷ . ⓡ

3

A: Is that your new homeroom teacher? 🎤 _____ ▷ .

B: Yes. We all have to be in class by 8:30. Late students get more homework. ⓡ

> 세이펜을 통해 각 상황에 맞는 말을 직접 녹음해
> 보고 확실히 익혔는지 확인해보세요.

📖 **[보기]** maybe 아마도 | keep -ing 계속 ~하다 **1.** get a haircut 머리를 자르다 **2.** let's ~하자 | take a picture 사진을 찍다 | ask 부탁하다 | someone 어떤 사람, 누군가 **3.** homeroom teacher 담임 선생님 | have to ~해야 한다 | more 더 많은

91
Track

It looks like an answer.

(그것은) ~ 같아 보여(~인 것 같아).

Say It! 물건이나 상황이 어때 보이는지 말할 때

Fill it! Listen to the track and fill in the blanks with the correct sentence number.

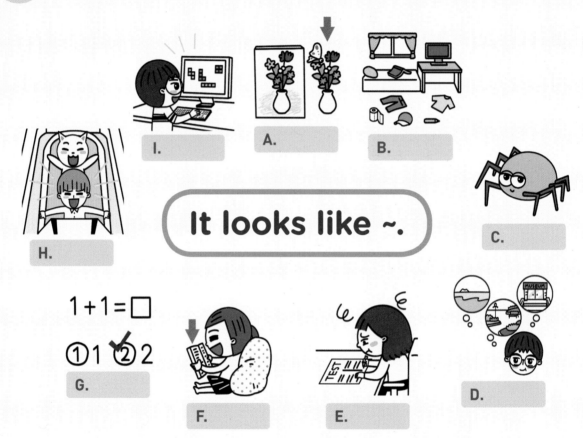

It looks like ~.

I. ____

A. ____

B. ____

H. ____

C. ____

1+1=☐
①1 ②2

G. ____

F. ____

E. ____

D. ____

---

805 It looks like an answer.

806 It looks like a spider.

807 It looks like a mess!

808 It looks like a fun game.

809 It looks like a difficult question.

810 It looks like a lot of fun!

811 It looks like a real one.

812 It looks like an interesting book.

813 It looks like a nice place to visit.

Study words & chunks!

⭐ Choose the correct words or chunks for each sentence and fill in the blanks. ▷

an answer

a lot of fun

a difficult question

an interesting book

a spider

a nice place to visit

a mess

a real one

a fun game

805 It looks like _____ . (답)

806 It looks like _____ . (거미)

807 It looks like _____ ! (엉망진창)

808 It looks like _____ . (재미있는 게임)

809 It looks like _____ . (어려운 문제)

810 It looks like _____ ! (큰 즐거움)

811 It looks like _____ . (진짜인 것)

812 It looks like _____ . (재미있는 책)

813 It looks like _____ . (방문하기 좋은 장소)

Guess it!

In each picture, what would he or she most likely say?
Using '**It looks like ~.**' make a sentence with the words or chunks below.

a spider	a real one	a difficult question
a fun game	an answer	a mess
a nice place to visit	a lot of fun	an interesting book

1.

_____

_____ .

2.

_____

_____ .

3.

_____

_____ .

Speak Up!

⭐ Complete the dialogues with the best sentence from this track.

> **보기**
>
> **A:** What are you playing? **It looks like a fun game**.
>
> **B:** Yes, it is really fun. I got it for my birthday. Do you want to try it?

1

A: Did you draw this apple? 🎤 _____ ▷.

B: Thanks. I like drawing real things.

Ⓡ

2

A: Look at your room. 🎤 _____ ▷!

B: It's my dog again. He always makes a mess.

A: Let's clean it together. I'll help you.

Ⓡ

3

A: Did you get an answer to number 3?

B: I didn't try it yet. But 🎤 _____ ▷.

A: Yes, it is. I didn't get the right answer.

Ⓡ

세이펜을 통해 각 상황에 맞는 말을 직접 녹음해 보고 확실히 익혔는지 확인해보세요.

📖 **[보기]** really 정말로 ㅣ get[got] 얻다[얻었다] ㅣ want to ~하고 싶다 ㅣ try 해 보다 **1.** like -ing ~하는 것을 좋아하다 **2.** make a mess 어지럽히다 ㅣ let's ~하자 **3.** yet 아직

memo 📝

memo 📝

memo ✒

EGU

THE EASIEST GRAMMAR & USAGE

EGU 시리즈 소개

EGU 서술형 기초 세우기

영단어&품사

서술형·문법의 기초가 되는
영단어와 품사 결합 학습

문장 형식

기본 동사 32개를 활용한
문장 형식별 학습

동사 써먹기

기본 동사 24개를 활용한
확장식 문장 쓰기 연습

EGU 서술형·문법 다지기

문법 써먹기

개정 교육 과정
중1 서술형·문법 완성

구문 써먹기

개정 교육 과정
중2, 중3 서술형·문법 완성

1 구문 — 판매 1위 '천일문' 콘텐츠를 활용하여 정확하고 다양한 구문 학습

끊어읽기   해석하기   문장 구조 분석   해설·해석 제공   단어 스크램블링   영작하기

2 문법·서술형 — 쎄듀의 모든 문법 문항을 활용하여 내신까지 해결하는 정교한 문법 유형 제공

객관식과 주관식의 결합   문법 포인트별 학습   보기를 활용한 집합 문항   내신대비 서술형   어법+서술형 문제

3 어휘 — 초·중·고·공무원까지 방대한 어휘량을 제공하며 오프라인 TEST 인쇄도 가능

영단어 카드 학습   단어 ↔ 뜻 유형   예문 활용 유형   단어 매칭 게임

4 선생님 보유 문항 이용

 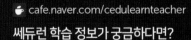

Online Test   OMR Test

cafe.naver.com/cedulearnteacher

쎄듀런 학습 정보가 궁금하다면?

쎄듀런 Cafe

· 쎄듀런 사용법 안내 & 학습법 공유
· 공지 및 문의사항 QA
· 할인 쿠폰 증정 등 이벤트 진행

Oh! MY SPEAKING
오! 마이 스피킹

대상	예비 초 ~ 초등 4학년
구성	**Student Book**
	Workbook, MP3 CD, Picture Cards 포함

① 레벨 1 ~ 6으로 세분화된 레벨링

② 의사소통 중심의 수업을 위해
교사와 학생 모두에게 최적화된 구성

③ 전략적 반복 학습의 나선형 시스템

④ 말하기를 중심으로
어휘, 문법까지 통합적 학습 가능

오! 마이 스피킹 교재 특징

**수준별 학습을 위한
6권 분류**

1권 / 2권	Early Beginners
3권 / 4권	Beginners
5권 / 6권	Pre-Intermediates

세이펜 적용 도서

세이펜으로
원어민 발음을
학습하고, 혼자서도
재미있게 학습해요!

**워크북 숙제도우미,
Christina(초코언니)**

워크북 속 QR코드와
세이펜으로
Christina의 음성을
들을 수 있어요!

천일문
sentence

WORKBOOK

with
세이펜

4

SAYPEN TV 쎄듀

초 등 코 치

천일문
sentence

✦ ✦ ✦

WORKBOOK

4

71
Track

I started feeling sick.

나는 ~하는 것을(~하기) 시작했어.

Master words & chunks!

Ⓐ 상자 안에 있는 단어 조각들을 화살표로 연결하여 이번 트랙에서 배운 표현을 만들어 보세요.

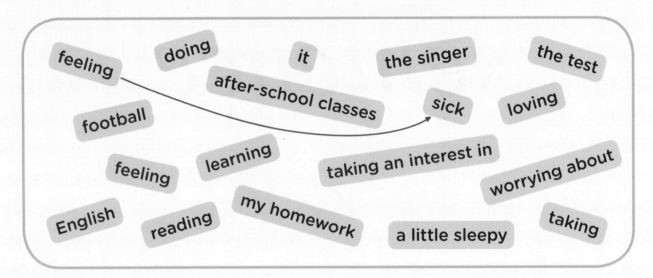

Ⓑ 상자에서 연결한 표현을 다시 한 번 써보고 뜻을 적어보세요.

Words & Chunks	뜻

Master sentences!

앞에서 복습한 표현을 사용하여 이번 트랙에서 배운 문장을 각 그림에 맞게 완성해보세요.

나는 ~하는 것을(~하기) 시작했어.

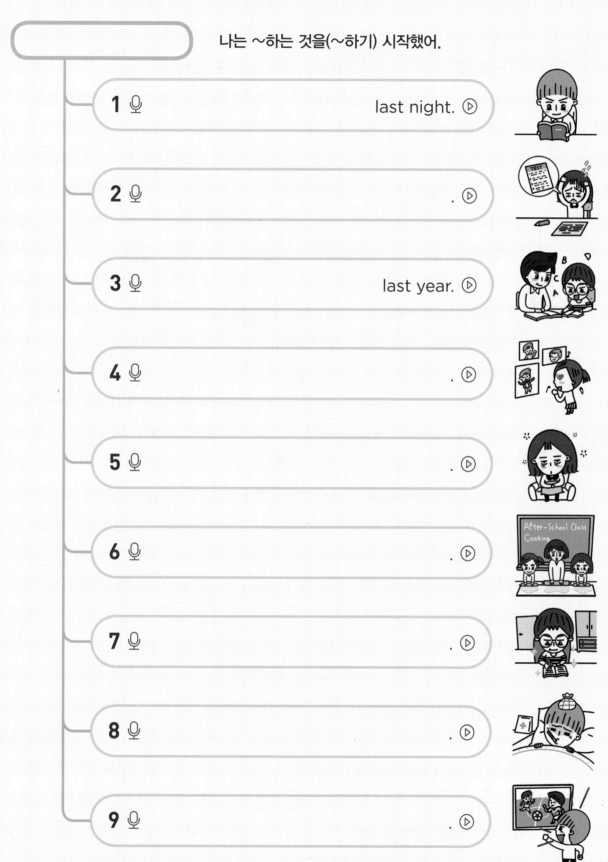

1 🎤   last night. ▷

2 🎤   . ▷

3 🎤   last year. ▷

4 🎤   . ▷

5 🎤   . ▷

6 🎤   . ▷

7 🎤   . ▷

8 🎤   . ▷

9 🎤   . ▷

72 Track

I began to get bored.

나는 ~하는 것을(~하기) 시작했어.

Master words & chunks!

Ⓐ 상자 안에 있는 단어 조각들을 화살표로 연결하여 이번 트랙에서 배운 표현을 만들어 보세요.

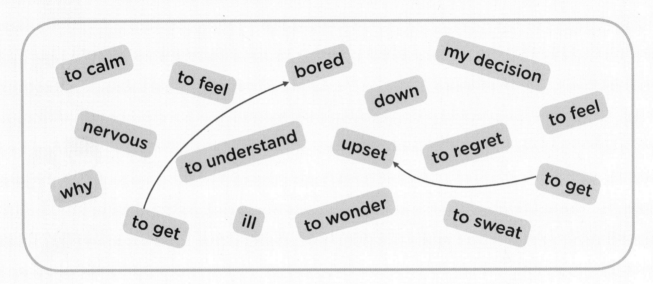

Ⓑ 상자에서 연결한 표현과 남는 단어 조각을 다시 한 번 써보고 뜻을 적어보세요.

Words & Chunks	뜻

Master sentences!

★ 앞에서 복습한 표현을 사용하여 이번 트랙에서 배운 문장을 각 그림에 맞게 완성해보세요.

나는 ~하는 것을(~하기) 시작했어.

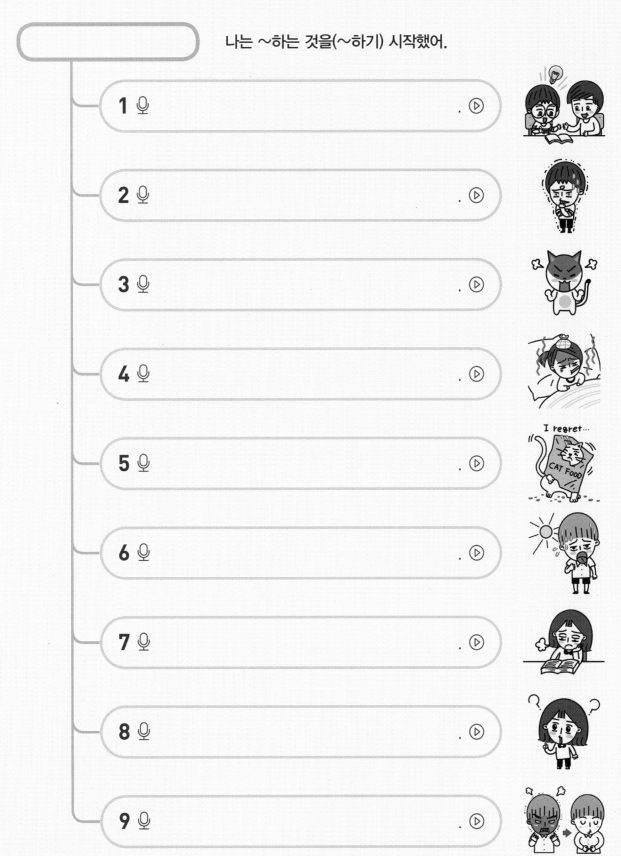

1

2

3

4

5

6

7

8

9

73 Track

Stop talking about that.

~하는 것을 그만해(그만 ~해).

Master words & chunks!

Ⓐ 상자 안에 있는 단어 조각들을 화살표로 연결하여 이번 트랙에서 배운 표현을 만들어 보세요.

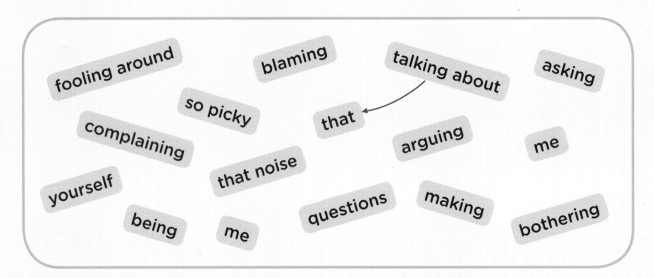

Ⓑ 상자에서 연결한 표현과 남는 단어 조각을 다시 한 번 써보고 뜻을 적어보세요.

Words & Chunks	뜻

Master sentences!

★ 앞에서 복습한 표현을 사용하여 이번 트랙에서 배운 문장을 각 그림에 맞게 완성해보세요.

┌─────────────────┐
│   │   ～하는 것을 그만해(그만 ～해).
└─────────────────┘

1 🎤 _____ . ▶

2 🎤 _____ . ▶

3 🎤 _____ . ▶

4 🎤 _____ ! ▶

5 🎤 _____ . ▶

6 🎤 _____ . ▶

7 🎤 _____ ! ▶

8 🎤 _____ . ▶

9 🎤 _____ . ▶

74 Track

I kept standing there.

나[우리]는 ~하는 것을 계속했어(계속 ~했어).

Master words & chunks!

Ⓐ 상자 안에 있는 단어 조각들을 화살표로 연결하여 이번 트랙에서 배운 표현을 만들어 보세요.

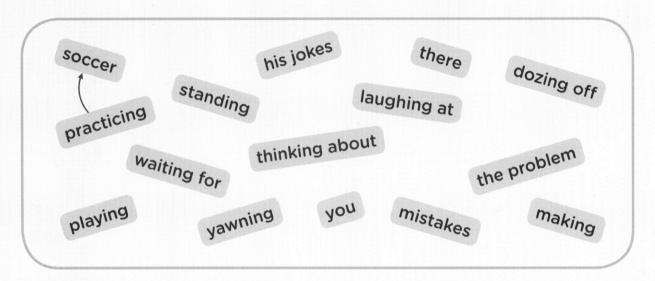

soccer · his jokes · there · dozing off · standing · laughing at · practicing · thinking about · waiting for · the problem · playing · yawning · you · mistakes · making

Ⓑ 상자에서 연결한 표현과 남는 단어 조각을 다시 한 번 써보고 뜻을 적어보세요.

Words & Chunks	뜻

Master sentences!

★ 앞에서 복습한 표현을 사용하여 이번 트랙에서 배운 문장을 각 그림에 맞게 완성해보세요.

나는 ～하는 것을 계속했어(계속 ～했어).

1 🎤 _____ . ▷

2 🎤 _____ . ▷

3 🎤 _____ . ▷

4 🎤 _____ all day. ▷

5 🎤 _____ . ▷

6 🎤 _____ . ▷

7 🎤 _____ . ▷

우리는 ～하는 것을 계속했어(계속 ～했어).

8 🎤 _____ for hours. ▷

9 🎤 _____ . ▷

75
Track

I want to watch TV.

나는 ~하기를 원해(~하고 싶어).

Master words & chunks!

ⓐ 상자 안에 있는 단어 조각들을 화살표로 연결하여 이번 트랙에서 배운 표현을 만들어 보세요.

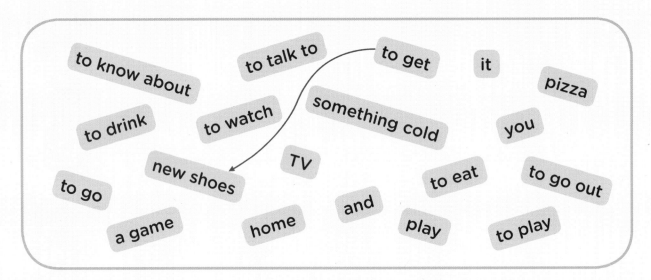

ⓑ 상자에서 연결한 표현을 다시 한 번 써보고 뜻을 적어보세요.

Words & Chunks	뜻

Master sentences!

⭐ 앞에서 복습한 표현을 사용하여 이번 트랙에서 배운 문장을 각 그림에 맞게 완성해보세요.

나는 ~하기를 원해(~하고 싶어).

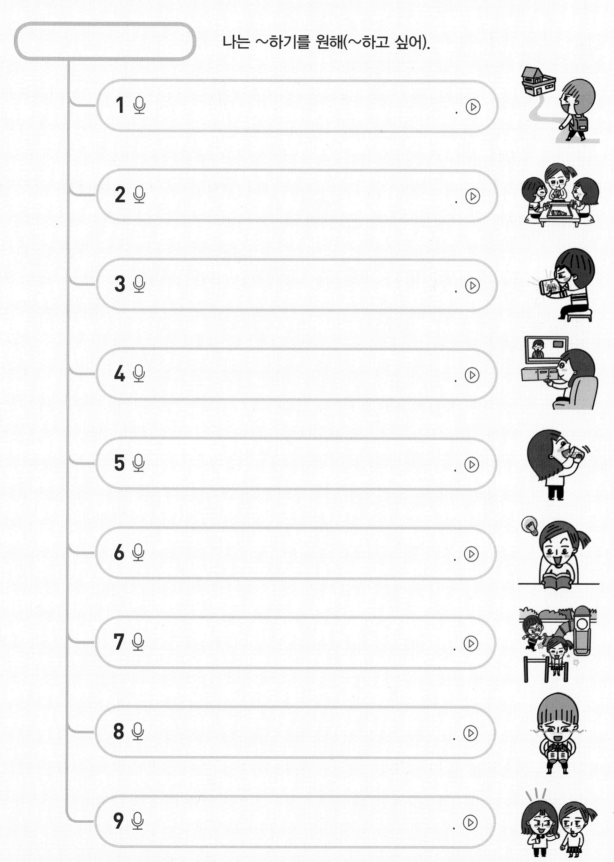

1 🎤   . ▷

2 🎤   . ▷

3 🎤   . ▷

4 🎤   . ▷

5 🎤   . ▷

6 🎤   . ▷

7 🎤   . ▷

8 🎤   . ▷

9 🎤   . ▷

76
Track

I don't want to go alone.

나는 ~하기를 원하지 않아(~하고 싶지 않아).

Master words & chunks!

Ⓐ 상자 안에 있는 단어 조각들을 화살표로 연결하여 이번 트랙에서 배운 표현을 만들어 보세요.

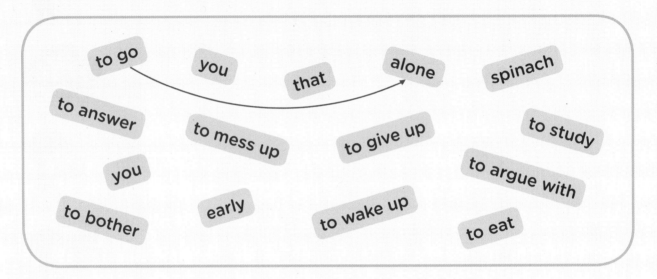

to go   you   that   alone   spinach

to answer   to mess up   to give up   to study

you   to argue with

to bother   early   to wake up   to eat

Ⓑ 상자에서 연결한 표현과 남는 단어 조각을 다시 한 번 써보고 뜻을 적어보세요.

Words & Chunks	뜻

Master sentences!

★ 앞에서 복습한 표현을 사용하여 이번 트랙에서 배운 문장을 각 그림에 맞게 완성해보세요.

나는 ～하기를 원하지 않아(～하고 싶지 않아).

1 🎤 _____ . ▷

2 🎤 _____ . ▷

3 🎤 _____ . ▷

4 🎤 _____ today. ▷

5 🎤 _____ . ▷

6 🎤 _____ . ▷

7 🎤 _____ . ▷

8 🎤 _____ . ▷

9 🎤 _____ . ▷

77 Track

I wanted to win the game.

나는 ～하기를 원했어(～하고 싶었어).

Master words & chunks!

Ⓐ 상자 안에 있는 단어 조각들을 화살표로 연결하여 이번 트랙에서 배운 표현을 만들어 보세요.

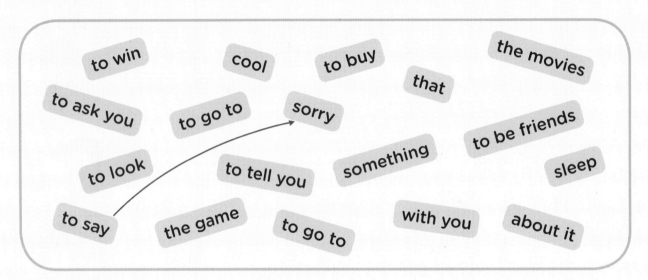

Ⓑ 상자에서 연결한 표현을 다시 한 번 써보고 뜻을 적어보세요.

Words & Chunks	뜻

Master sentences!

앞에서 복습한 표현을 사용하여 이번 트랙에서 배운 문장을 각 그림에 맞게 완성해보세요.

나는 ～하기를 원했어(～하고 싶었어).

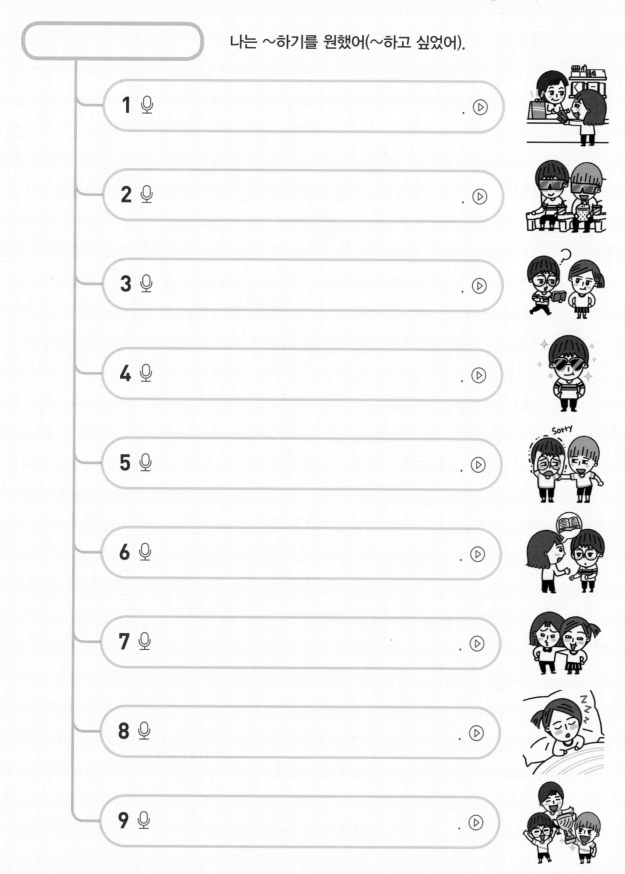

78 Track

I like to travel.

나는 ~하는 것을 좋아해.

Master words & chunks!

Ⓐ 상자 안에 있는 단어 조각들을 화살표로 연결하여 이번 트랙에서 배운 표현을 만들어 보세요.

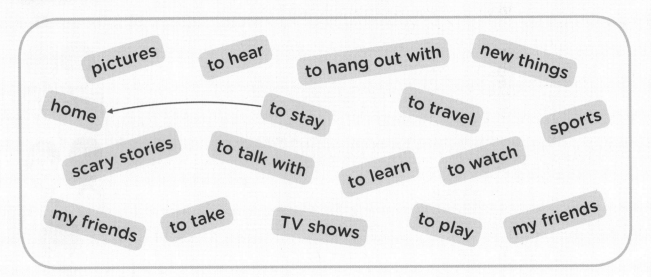

Ⓑ 상자에서 연결한 표현과 남는 단어 조각을 다시 한 번 써보고 뜻을 적어보세요.

Words & Chunks	뜻

Master sentences!

⭐ 앞에서 복습한 표현을 사용하여 이번 트랙에서 배운 문장을 각 그림에 맞게 완성해보세요.

나는 ~하는 것을 좋아해.

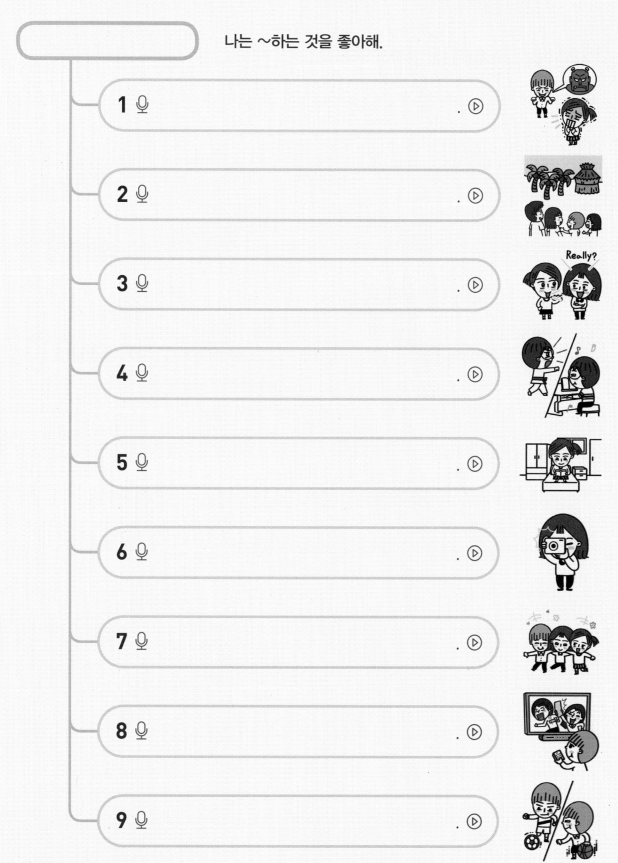

79 Track

I need to talk to you.

나는 ∼하는 것이 필요해(∼해야 해).

Master words & chunks!

Ⓐ 상자 안에 있는 단어 조각들을 화살표로 연결하여 이번 트랙에서 배운 표현을 만들어 보세요.

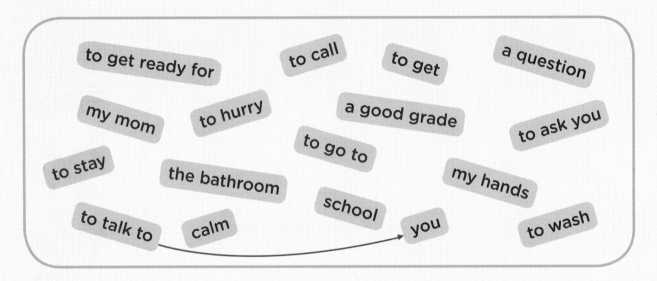

Ⓑ 상자에서 연결한 표현과 남는 단어 조각을 다시 한 번 써보고 뜻을 적어보세요.

Words & Chunks	뜻

Master sentences!

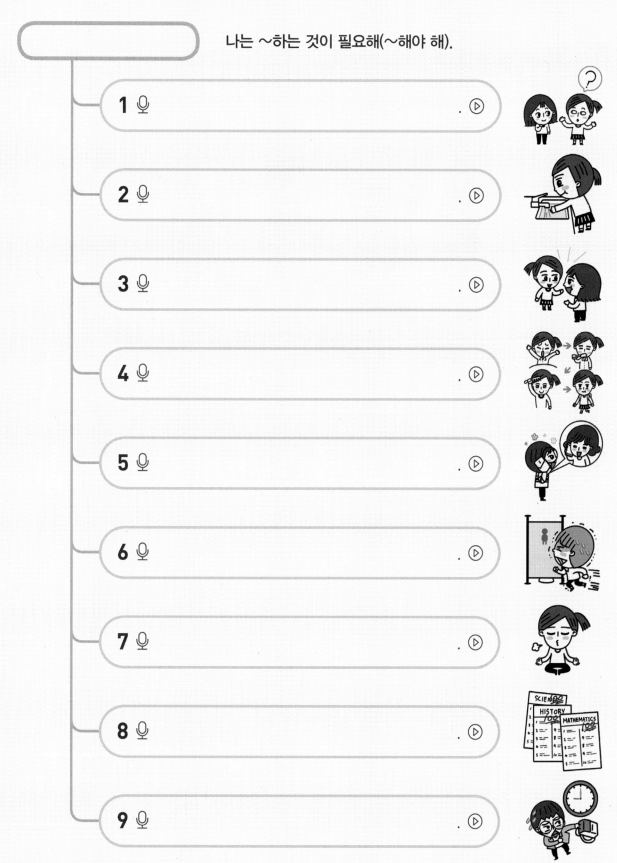

★ 앞에서 복습한 표현을 사용하여 이번 트랙에서 배운 문장을 각 그림에 맞게 완성해보세요.

나는 ~하는 것이 필요해(~해야 해).

1 🎤   . ▷

2 🎤   . ▷

3 🎤   . ▷

4 🎤   . ▷

5 🎤   . ▷

6 🎤   . ▷

7 🎤   . ▷

8 🎤   . ▷

9 🎤   . ▷

80 Track

I tried to call you.

나는 ~하려고 (노력)했어.

Master words & chunks!

Ⓐ 상자 안에 있는 단어 조각들을 화살표로 연결하여 이번 트랙에서 배운 표현을 만들어 보세요.

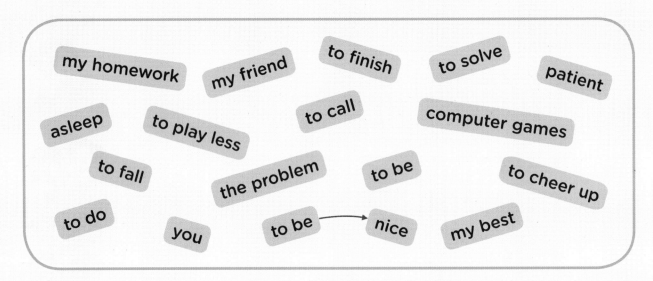

my homework   my friend   to finish   to solve   patient

asleep   to play less   to call   computer games

to fall   the problem   to be   to cheer up

to do   you   to be → nice   my best

Ⓑ 상자에서 연결한 표현을 다시 한 번 써보고 뜻을 적어보세요.

Words & Chunks	뜻

Master sentences!

★ 앞에서 복습한 표현을 사용하여 이번 트랙에서 배운 문장을 각 그림에 맞게 완성해보세요.

나는 ~하려고 (노력)했어.

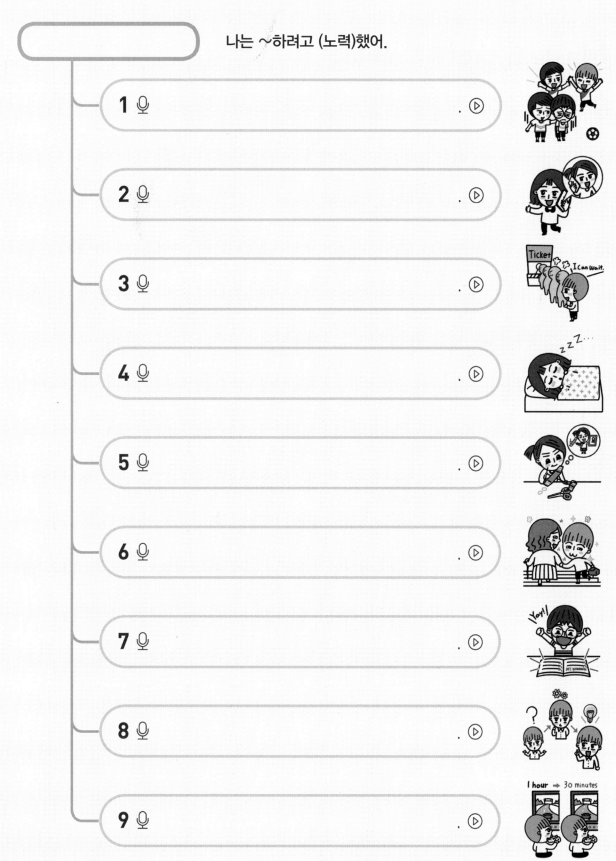

1 ⬥ _____ . ▷

2 ⬥ _____ . ▷

3 ⬥ _____ . ▷

4 ⬥ _____ . ▷

5 ⬥ _____ . ▷

6 ⬥ _____ . ▷

7 ⬥ _____ . ▷

8 ⬥ _____ . ▷

9 ⬥ _____ . ▷

81 Track

I'm supposed to clean my room.

나는 ～하기로 되어 있어(～해야 해).

Master words & chunks!

Ⓐ 상자 안에 있는 단어 조각들을 화살표로 연결하여 이번 트랙에서 배운 표현을 만들어 보세요.

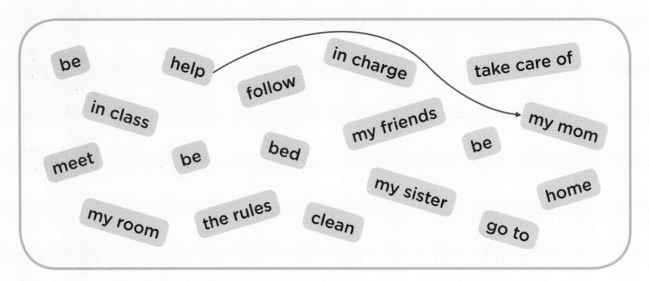

Ⓑ 상자에서 연결한 표현을 다시 한 번 써보고 뜻을 적어보세요.

Words & Chunks	뜻

Master sentences!

★ 앞에서 복습한 표현을 사용하여 이번 트랙에서 배운 문장을 각 그림에 맞게 완성해보세요.

나는 ～하기로 되어 있어(～해야 해).

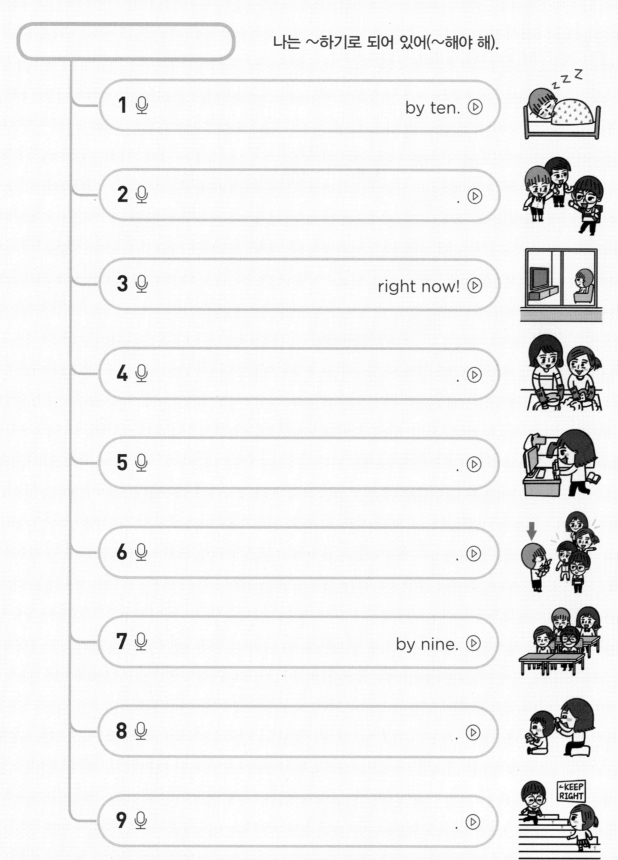

1 🎤   by ten. ▷

2 🎤   . ▷

3 🎤   right now! ▷

4 🎤   . ▷

5 🎤   . ▷

6 🎤   . ▷

7 🎤   by nine. ▷

8 🎤   . ▷

9 🎤   . ▷

It's time to get ready.

~할 시간이야.

Master words & chunks!

Ⓐ 상자 안에 있는 단어 조각들을 화살표로 연결하여 이번 트랙에서 배운 표현을 만들어 보세요.

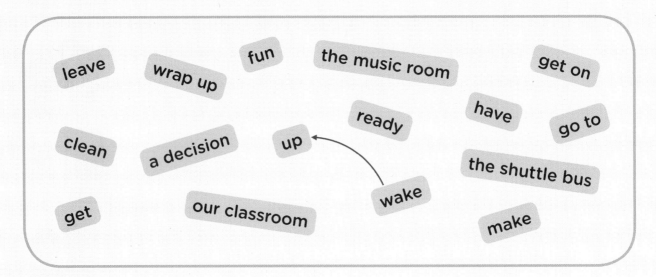

Ⓑ 상자에서 연결한 표현과 남는 단어 조각을 다시 한 번 써보고 뜻을 적어보세요.

Words & Chunks	뜻

Master sentences!

⭐ 앞에서 복습한 표현을 사용하여 이번 트랙에서 배운 문장을 각 그림에 맞게 완성해보세요.

~할 시간이야.

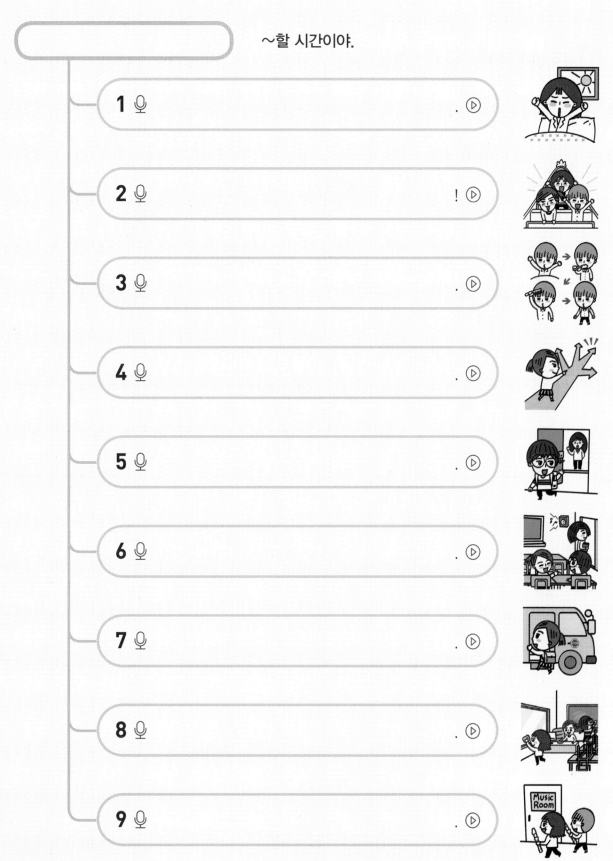

83 Track

Do you know how to do it?

너는 ~하는 법을(~할 줄) 알아?

Master words & chunks!

Ⓐ 상자 안에 있는 단어 조각들을 화살표로 연결하여 이번 트랙에서 배운 표현을 만들어 보세요.

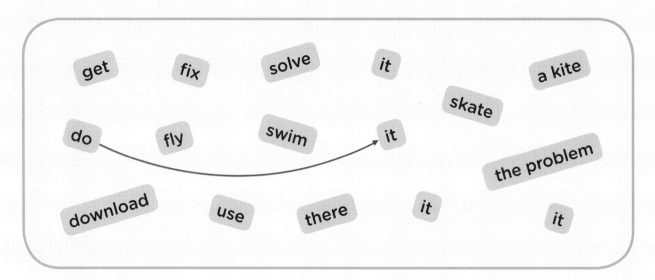

Ⓑ 상자에서 연결한 표현과 남는 단어 조각을 다시 한 번 써보고 뜻을 적어보세요.

Words & Chunks	뜻

Master sentences!

★ 앞에서 복습한 표현을 사용하여 이번 트랙에서 배운 문장을 각 그림에 맞게 완성해보세요.

너는 ~하는 법을(~할 줄) 알아?

1 🎤 _____ ? ▷

2 🎤 _____ ? ▷

3 🎤 _____ ? ▷

4 🎤 _____ ? ▷

5 🎤 _____ ? ▷

6 🎤 _____ ? ▷

7 🎤 _____ ? ▷

8 🎤 _____ ? ▷

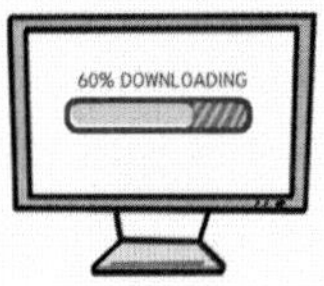

9 🎤 _____ ? ▷

84 Track
I don't know what to say.

나는 무엇을 ～해야 할지 모르겠어.

Master words & chunks!

⭐ 아래 적혀 있는 한글 뜻에 알맞은 단어를 상자 안에서 찾아 완성하고, 주어진 영어 표현에는 알맞은 한글 뜻을 쓰세요.

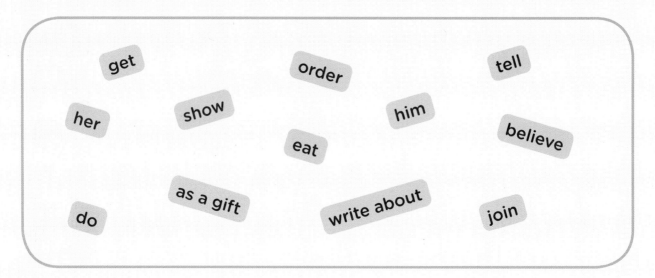

Words & Chunks	뜻
	하다
pick	
	주문하다
	～에 대해 쓰다
	그에게 말하다
say	
wear	
	믿다
	그녀에게 선물로 ～을 주다

Master sentences!

★ 앞에서 복습한 표현을 사용하여 이번 트랙에서 배운 문장을 각 그림에 맞게 완성해보세요.

나는 무엇을 ~해야 할지 모르겠어.

1 🎤 . ▷

2 🎤 . ▷

3 🎤 . ▷

4 🎤 . ▷

5 🎤 next. ▷

6 🎤 . ▷

7 🎤 . ▷

8 🎤 . ▷

9 🎤 . ▷

85
Track

He seems to be busy.

그[그녀]는 ~하는 것처럼 보여(~하는 것 같아).

Master words & chunks!

Ⓐ 상자 안에 있는 단어 조각들을 화살표로 연결하여 이번 트랙에서 배운 표현을 만들어 보세요.

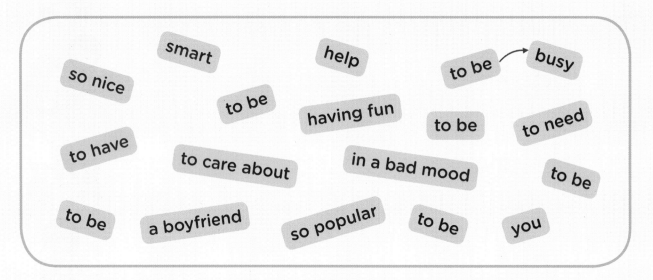

smart help to be → busy so nice to be having fun to be to need to have to care about in a bad mood to be to be a boyfriend so popular to be you

Ⓑ 상자에서 연결한 표현과 남는 단어 조각을 다시 한 번 써보고 뜻을 적어보세요.

Words & Chunks	뜻

Master sentences!

★ 앞에서 복습한 표현을 사용하여 이번 트랙에서 배운 문장을 각 그림에 맞게 완성해보세요.

그는 ~하는 것처럼 보여(~하는 것 같아).

1 🎤 . ▷

2 🎤 . ▷

3 🎤 . ▷

4 🎤 . ▷

그녀는 ~하는 것처럼 보여(~하는 것 같아).

5 🎤 . ▷

6 🎤 . ▷

7 🎤 . ▷

8 🎤 . ▷

9 🎤 . ▷

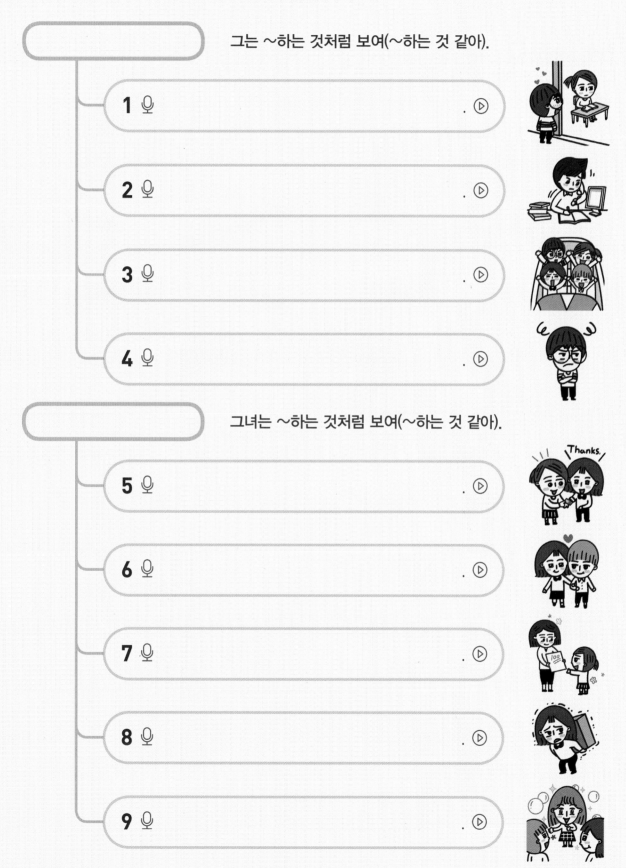

86
Track

You look tired.

너는 ~해 보여.

Master words & chunks!

⭐ 아래 적혀 있는 한글 뜻에 알맞은 단어를 상자 안에서 찾아 완성하고, 주어진 영어 표현에는 알맞은 한글 뜻을 쓰세요.

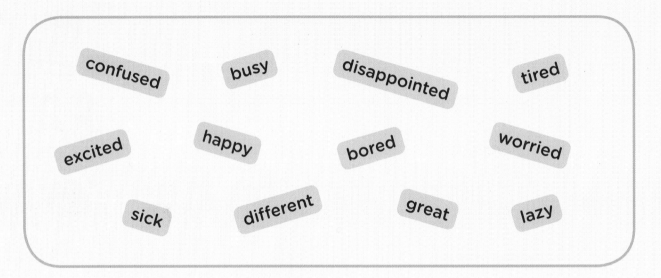

confused　busy　disappointed　tired

excited　happy　bored　worried

sick　different　great　lazy

Words & Chunks	뜻
surprised	
	지루해하는
	멋진
	행복한
	걱정스러운
	혼란스러운, 헷갈리는
angry	
	피곤한
	신이 난

Master sentences!

★ 앞에서 복습한 표현을 사용하여 이번 트랙에서 배운 문장을 각 그림에 맞게 완성해보세요.

너는 ～해 보여.

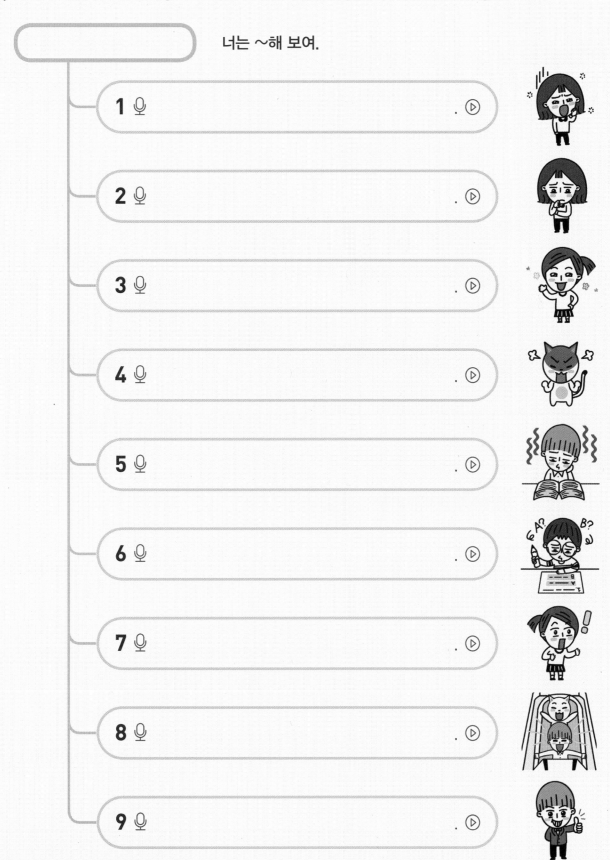

1 🎤 .

2 🎤 .

3 🎤 .

4 🎤 .

5 🎤 .

6 🎤 .

7 🎤 .

8 🎤 .

9 🎤 .

87
Track

I feel better.

나는 ~한 느낌이야(기분이야).

Master words & chunks!

⭐ 아래 적혀 있는 한글 뜻에 알맞은 단어를 상자 안에서 찾아 완성하고, 주어진 영어 표현에는 알맞은 한글 뜻을 쓰세요.

good sad upset proud happy better sleepy chilly angry hungry comfortable nervous

Words & Chunks	뜻
scared	
	몸이 나아진, 기분이 나아진
	편안한
	슬픈
	자랑스러운
	긴장한
embarrassed	
	추운, 쌀쌀한
sick	

Master sentences!

⭐ 앞에서 복습한 표현을 사용하여 이번 트랙에서 배운 문장을 각 그림에 맞게 완성해보세요.

나는 ～한 느낌이야(기분이야).

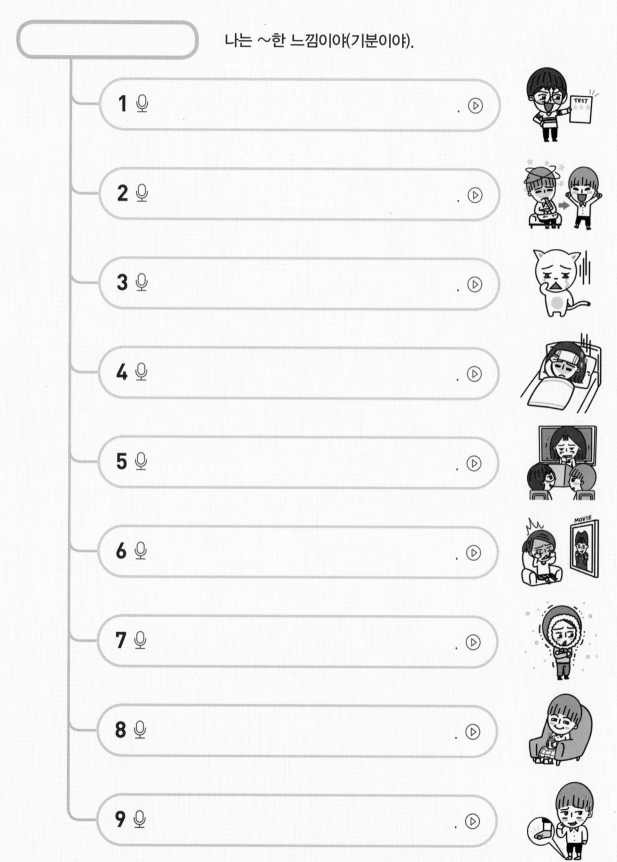

1 🎤 .

2 🎤 .

3 🎤 .

4 🎤 .

5 🎤 .

6 🎤 .

7 🎤 .

8 🎤 .

9 🎤 .

88
Track

I got hungry.

나는 ~됐어.

Master words & chunks!

⭐ 아래 적혀 있는 한글 뜻에 알맞은 단어를 상자 안에서 찾아 완성하고, 주어진 영어 표현에는 알맞은 한글 뜻을 쓰세요.

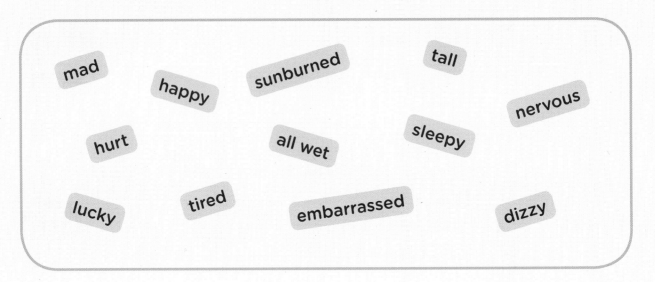

Words & Chunks	뜻
	어지러운
	다친
	다 젖은
carsick	
	햇볕에 심하게 탄
	몹시 화가 난
hungry	
	운이 좋은
	긴장한

Master sentences!

★ 앞에서 복습한 표현을 사용하여 이번 트랙에서 배운 문장을 각 그림에 맞게 완성해보세요.

나는 ～됐어.

1 🎤 . ▷

2 🎤 . ▷

3 🎤 . ▷

4 🎤 . ▷

5 🎤 . ▷

6 🎤 . ▷

7 🎤 . ▷

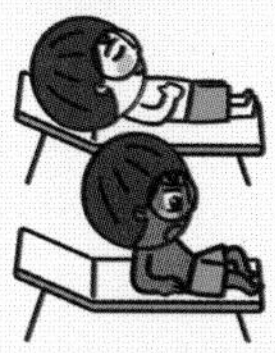

8 🎤 . ▷

9 🎤 . ▷

89
Track

I'm getting bored.

나는 점점 ~해지고 있어.

Master words & chunks!

⭐ 아래 적혀 있는 한글 뜻에 알맞은 단어를 상자 안에서 찾아 완성하고, 주어진 영어 표현에는 알맞은 한글 뜻을 쓰세요.

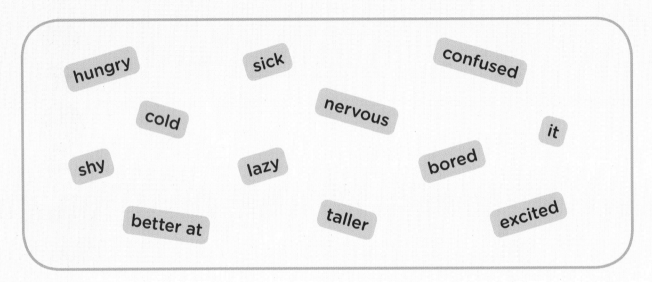

Words & Chunks	뜻
	키가 더 큰
	긴장한
	혼란스러운, 헷갈리는
	그것을 더 잘하는
	배고픈
	추운
full	
tired of waiting	
	지루한

Master sentences!

★ 앞에서 복습한 표현을 사용하여 이번 트랙에서 배운 문장을 각 그림에 맞게 완성해보세요.

나는 점점 ~해지고 있어.

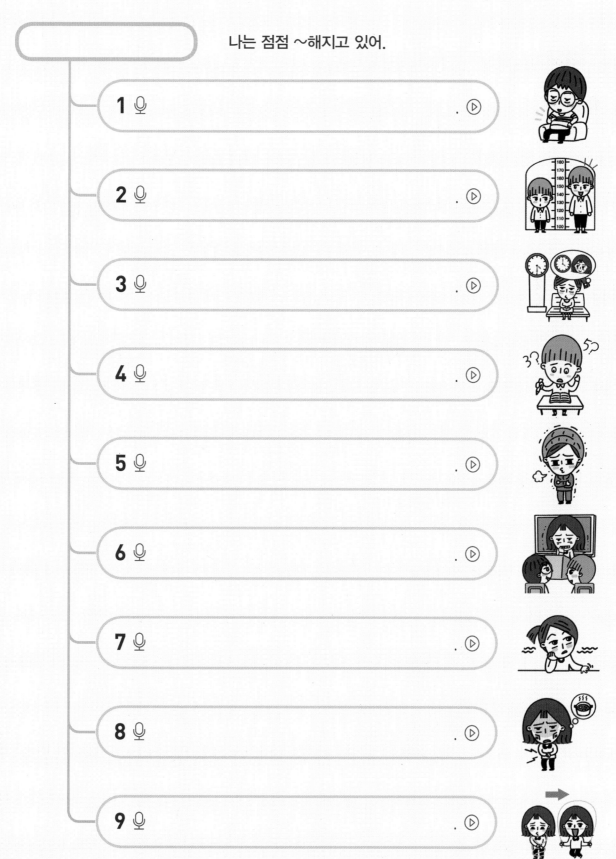

1 🎤 _____ .▷

2 🎤 _____ .▷

3 🎤 _____ .▷

4 🎤 _____ .▷

5 🎤 _____ .▷

6 🎤 _____ .▷

7 🎤 _____ .▷

8 🎤 _____ .▷

9 🎤 _____ .▷

90 Track

She seems so busy.

그[그녀]는 ~인 것처럼 보여(~인 것 같아).

Master words & chunks!

⭐ 아래 적혀 있는 한글 뜻에 알맞은 단어를 상자 안에서 찾아 완성하고, 주어진 영어 표현에는 알맞은 한글 뜻을 쓰세요.

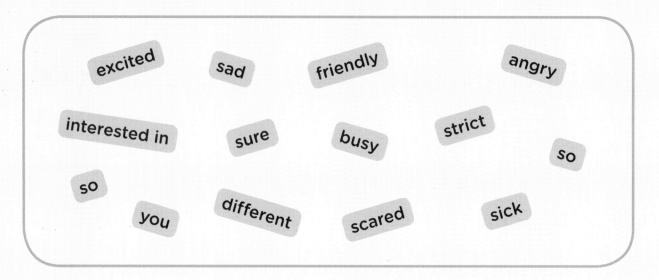

Words & Chunks	뜻
	너에게 관심이 있는
	아픈
	엄격한
strange	
	친절한
smart	
	매우 확신하는
	다른
	매우 바쁜

Master sentences!

⭐ 앞에서 복습한 표현을 사용하여 이번 트랙에서 배운 문장을 각 그림에 맞게 완성해보세요.

그는 ~인 것처럼 보여(~인 것 같아).

1. 🎤 _____ today. ▶

2. 🎤 _____ . ▶

3. 🎤 _____ . ▶

4. 🎤 _____ . ▶

5. 🎤 _____ . ▶

그녀는 ~인 것처럼 보여(~인 것 같아).

6. 🎤 _____ . ▶

7. 🎤 _____ . ▶

8. 🎤 _____ . ▶

9. 🎤 _____ . ▶

91

Track

It looks like an answer.

(그것은) ~ 같아 보여(~인 것 같아).

Master words & chunks!

⭐ 아래 적혀 있는 한글 뜻에 알맞은 단어를 상자 안에서 찾아 완성하고, 주어진 영어 표현에는 알맞은 한글 뜻을 쓰세요.

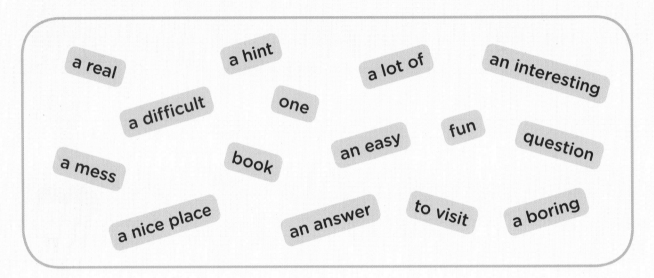

Words & Chunks	뜻
	엉망진창
	큰 즐거움
	답
	진짜인 것
	재미있는 책
	방문하기 좋은 장소
a spider	
a fun game	
	어려운 문제

Master sentences!

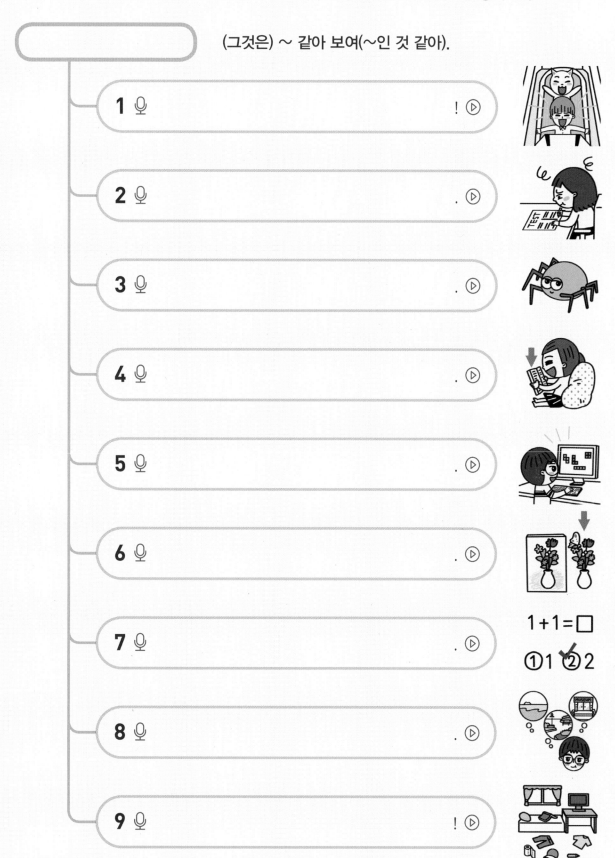

★ 앞에서 복습한 표현을 사용하여 이번 트랙에서 배운 문장을 각 그림에 맞게 완성해보세요.

(그것은) ~ 같아 보여(~인 것 같아).

1 🎤 _____ ! ▷

2 🎤 _____ . ▷

3 🎤 _____ . ▷

4 🎤 _____ . ▷

5 🎤 _____ . ▷

6 🎤 _____ . ▷

7 🎤 _____ . ▷

8 🎤 _____ . ▷

9 🎤 _____ ! ▷

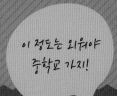

초등코치

천일문 *voca&story*

1,001개의 초등 필수 어휘와 짧은 스토리

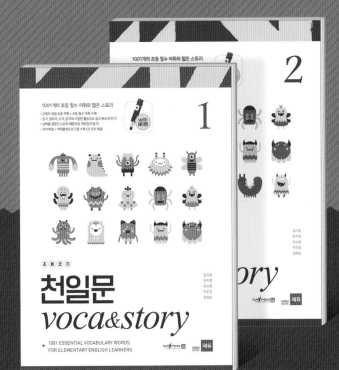

이 정도는 외워야
중학교 가지!

스토리와 어휘의 결합
어휘, 재미있는
암기가 가능하다!

1 | 교육부 권장 어휘 + 초등 필수 어휘 1,001개 완벽 정리

2 | 유닛별로 10개 단어씩 묶어 쉽고 빠르게 암기

3 | 짧은 스토리 예문을 통해 재미있게 암기

4 | Workbook 및 무료 부가서비스 제공

5 | 세이펜(음성 재생장치)을 활용해 실시간으로 듣고 따라 말하는 효율적인 학습 가능

녹음 기능을 통한 쉐도잉, Review Test 게임을 통한 재미있는 단어 암기!

with
세이펜

* 기존 보유하고 계신 세이펜으로도 핀파일 업데이트 후 사용 가능합니다.

• 연계 & 후속 학습에 좋은 초등코치 천일문 시리즈 •

초등코치 천일문
SENTENCE 1, 2, 3, 4, 5
-
1,001개 통문장
암기로 영어의 기초 완성

초등코치 천일문
GRAMMAR 1, 2, 3
-
1,001개 예문으로
배우는 초등 영문법

쎄듀북닷컴(www.cedubook.com)에서 부가 자료를 무료로 다운로드할 수 있습니다.

쎄듀

쎄듀 초등 커리큘럼

	예비초	초1	초2	초3	초4	초5	초6
구문		신간 천일문 365 일력 |초1-3| 교육부 지정 초등 필수 영어 문장		초등코치 천일문 SENTENCE 1001개 통문장 암기로 완성하는 초등 영어의 기초			
문법			신간 왓츠 Grammar Start 시리즈 초등 기초 영문법 입문		초등코치 천일문 GRAMMAR 1001개 예문으로 배우는 초등 영문법		
						신간 왓츠 Grammar Plus 시리즈 초등 필수 영문법 마무리	
독해					신간 왓츠 리딩 70 / 80 / 90 / 100 A / B 쉽고 재미있게 완성되는 영어 독해력		
어휘				초등코치 천일문 VOCA&STORY 1001개의 초등 필수 어휘와 짧은 스토리			
		패턴으로 말하는 초등 필수 영단어 1 / 2		문장 패턴으로 완성하는 초등 필수 영단어			
ELT	Oh! My PHONICS 1 / 2 / 3 / 4 유·초등학생을 위한 첫 영어 파닉스						
		Oh! My SPEAKING 1 / 2 / 3 / 4 / 5 / 6 핵심 문장 패턴으로 더욱 쉬운 영어 말하기					
		Oh! My GRAMMAR 1 / 2 / 3 쓰기로 완성하는 첫 초등 영문법					

쎄듀 중등 커리큘럼

	예비중	중1	중2	중3
구문		신간 천일문 STARTER 1 / 2		중등 필수 구문 & 문법 총정리
문법		천일문 GRAMMAR LEVEL 1 / 2 / 3		예문 중심 문법 기본서
		GRAMMAR Q Starter 1, 2 / Intermediate 1, 2 / Advanced 1, 2		학기별 문법 기본서
		잘 풀리는 영문법 1 / 2 / 3		문제 중심 문법 적용서
		GRAMMAR PIC 1 / 2 / 3 / 4		이해가 쉬운 도식화된 문법서
			1센치 영문법	1권으로 핵심 문법 정리
문법+어법			첫단추 BASIC 문법·어법편 1 / 2	문법·어법의 기초
문법+쓰기	EGU 영단어&품사 / 문장 형식 / 동사 써먹기 / 문법 써먹기 / 구문 써먹기			서술형 기초 세우기와 문법 다지기
				올씀 1 기본 문장 PATTERN 내신 서술형 기본 문장 학습
쓰기		거침없이 Writing LEVEL 1 / 2 / 3		중등 교과서 내신 기출 서술형
		개정 중학 영어 쓰작 1 / 2 / 3		중등 교과서 패턴 드릴 서술형
어휘		어휘끝 중학 필수편	중학 필수어휘 1000개	어휘끝 중학 마스터편 고난도 중학어휘 +고등기초 어휘 1000개
독해		Reading Relay Starter 1, 2 / Challenger 1, 2 / Master 1, 2		타교과 연계 배경 지식 독해
		READING Q Starter 1, 2 / Intermediate 1, 2 / Advanced 1, 2		예측/추론/요약 사고력 독해
독해전략			리딩 플랫폼 1 / 2 / 3	논픽션 지문 독해
독해유형			Reading 16 LEVEL 1 / 2 / 3	수능 유형 맛보기 + 내신 대비
			첫단추 BASIC 독해편 1 / 2	수능 유형 독해 입문
듣기		Listening Q 유형편 / 1 / 2 / 3		유형별 듣기 전략 및 실전 대비
		쎄듀 빠르게 중학영어듣기 모의고사 1 / 2 / 3		교육청 듣기평가 대비

초 등 코 치

천일문
sentence

✦ ✦ ✦

정답과 해설

4

Track | **71** I started feeling sick.

p.14

Fill it!

A. 626 B. 628 C. 629 D. 633 E. 630
F. 627 G. 631 H. 625 I. 632

해석

625 나는 아프기 시작했어.
626 나는 조금 졸리기 시작했어.
627 나는 그 가수가 정말 좋아지기 시작했어.
628 나는 내 숙제를 하기 시작했어.
629 나는 어젯밤에 그것을 읽기 시작했어.
630 나는 시험에 대해 걱정하기 시작했어.
631 나는 작년에 영어를 배우기 시작했어.
632 나는 방과 후 수업을 듣기 시작했어.
633 나는 축구에 흥미를 갖기 시작했어.

Study words & chunks!

625 feeling sick
626 feeling a little sleepy
627 loving the singer
628 doing my homework
629 reading it
630 worrying about the test
631 learning English
632 taking after-school classes
633 taking an interest in football

Guess it!

1. I started loving the singer
2. I started learning English
3. I started feeling sick

Speak Up!

보기

A: 나는 시험이 걱정되기 시작했어.
B: 긴장 풀어. 열 문제뿐이잖아. 괜찮을 거야.

1. I started reading it
   A: 그 책은 무엇에 관한 거야? 책 표지가 재미있어 보여.
   B: 나는 아직 그것에 대해 잘 몰라. **나는 어젯밤에 그걸 읽기 시작했거든.**

2. I started taking after-school classes
   A: 네가 정말 이 로봇을 만들었어?
   B: 응, 내가 수업 시간에 만들었어. **나는 방과 후 수업을 듣기 시작했거든.**
   A: 나도 그 수업을 듣고 싶어! 너무 재미있어 보여.

3. I started feeling a little sleepy
   A: 나는 조금 졸리기 시작했어.
   B: 수업이 거의 끝나가. 아직 잠들지 마.

Track | **72** I began to get bored.

p.18

Fill it!

A. 641 B. 642 C. 639 D. 636 E. 637
F. 635 G. 640 H. 634 I. 638

해석

634 나는 이해하기 시작했어.
635 나는 진정하기 시작했어.
636 나는 화가 나기 시작했어.
637 나는 지루해지기 시작했어.
638 나는 아프기 시작했어.
639 나는 긴장하기 시작했어.
640 나는 땀을 흘리기 시작했어.
641 나는 왜인지 궁금하기 시작했어.
   (→나는 이유가 궁금하기 시작했어.)
642 나는 내 결정을 후회하기 시작했어.

Study words & chunks!

634 to understand
635 to calm down
636 to get upset

637 to get bored
638 to feel ill
639 to feel nervous
640 to sweat
641 to wonder why
642 to regret my decision

Guess it!

1. I began to get upset
2. I began to regret my decision
3. I began to sweat

Speak Up!

보기

A: 듣기 시험 어떻게 봤어?
B: **나는 긴장하기 시작했어.** 그래서 실수를 좀 했어.

1. I began to get bored

A: 나 피아노 수업 그만뒀어.
B: 왜? 너 좋아했잖아.
A: **나는 지루해지기 시작했거든.** 더 재미있는 걸 배울 거야.

2. I began to feel ill

A: 어제 왜 학교 안 왔어?
B: **나는 아프기 시작했어.** 그래서 집에 있어야 했어.

3. I began to wonder why

A: 인터넷에서 뭐 찾고 있어?
B: 자동차가 코코넛을 사용해서 달릴 수 있다고 들었어. 그리고 **이유가 궁금하기 시작했어.**
A: 그래서, 뭘 알아냈어?

Track 73 Stop talking about that.

p.22

Fill it!

A. 646   B. 649   C. 645   D. 643   E. 648
F. 650   G. 647   H. 644   I. 651

해석

643 그것에 대해 그만 이야기해.
　　(→그 얘기는 그만해.)
644 나에게 질문 좀 그만해.
645 그만 까다롭게 굴어!
646 그만 시끄럽게 해.
647 그만 다퉈.
648 불평 그만해! (→그만 좀 투덜거려!)
649 나 좀 그만 귀찮게 해.
650 장난 좀 그만 쳐.
651 너 자신을 그만 탓해.

Study words & chunks!

643 talking about that
644 asking me questions
645 being so picky
646 making that noise
647 arguing

648 complaining
649 bothering me
650 fooling around
651 blaming yourself

Guess it!

1. Stop bothering me
2. Stop talking about that
3. Stop making that noise

Speak Up!

보기

A: 나는 햄 샌드위치 먹을 거야. 너는?
B: 모르겠어. 나는 오이도 싫어하고, 당근도, 치즈도... 그리고 또 못 먹는 게...
A: **그만 까다롭게 굴어!**

1. Stop asking me questions

A: 답이 뭐야? 어떻게 풀었어? 너한테는 그거 쉬웠어?
B: **나한테 질문 좀 그만해.** 네 모든 질문에 대답할 수 없어.
A: 미안해. 하나하나씩 물어볼게.

2. Stop complaining

A: 나는 비 오는 날이 싫어. 내 옷이 비에 항상 젖는단 말이야. 게다가, 축구도 할 수 없잖아!

B: **그만 좀 투덜거려!** 비가 영원히 오는 게 아니잖아.

3. Stop blaming yourself

A: 나는 상대 팀에 두 골을 넣어버렸어. 모두가 날 싫어할 거야.

B: 그렇지 않을 거야. **너 자신을 그만 탓해.** 모두가 실수하잖아.

Track | 74 I kept standing there.

p.26

Fill it!

A. 659 B. 653 C. 656 D. 658 E. 657
F. 660 G. 655 H. 652 I. 654

> 해석
>
> 652 나는 계속 그곳에 서 있었어.
> 653 나는 계속 너를 기다렸어.
> 654 나는 계속 실수를 했어.
> 655 우리는 몇 시간 동안 계속 놀았어.
> 656 우리는 계속 축구를 연습했어.
> 657 나는 계속 꾸벅꾸벅 졸았어.
> 658 나는 온종일 계속 하품했어.
> 659 나는 계속 그 문제에 대해 생각했어.
> 660 나는 계속 그의 농담에 웃었어.

Study words & chunks!

652 standing there
653 waiting for you
654 making mistakes
655 playing
656 practicing soccer
657 dozing off   658 yawning
659 thinking about the problem
660 laughing at his jokes

Guess it!

1. I kept yawning
2. I kept laughing at his jokes
3. I kept waiting for you

Speak Up!

> 보기
>
> A: 너 어제 그 애들이랑 재미있게 놀았어?
> B: 응. **우리는 몇 시간 동안 계속 놀았어.**
> A: 좋았겠다. 나도 다음번엔 너희와 함께할게.

1. I kept making mistakes

A: 대회 어땠어? 너 잘했어?

B: 아니. **나는 계속 실수를 했어.** 나 너무 긴장됐거든!

2. I kept dozing off

A: 일어나! 우리 거의 다 왔어.

B: 아, 그렇구나. **나는 계속 꾸벅꾸벅 졸았어.**

A: 너 피곤한 거 알지만, 일어나! 우리 곧 내려야 해.

3. I kept thinking about the problem

A: 너 답 찾았어?

B: 아니. **계속 그 문제에 대해 생각했는데,** 아직도 모르겠어.

Track | 75 I want to watch TV.

p.30

Fill it!

A. 662 B. 661 C. 666 D. 667 E. 664
F. 668 G. 663 H. 665 I. 669

> 해석
>
> 661 나는 피자를 먹고 싶어.
> 662 나는 집에 가고 싶어.
> 663 나는 TV를 보고 싶어.

664 나는 게임 하고 싶어.

665 나는 나가서 놀고 싶어.

666 나는 너에게 이야기하고 싶어.

667 나는 새 신발을 갖고 싶어.

668 나는 그것에 대해 알고 싶어.

669 나는 시원한 것을 마시고 싶어.

Study words & chunks!

661 to eat pizza   662 to go home

663 to watch TV

664 to play a game

665 to go out and play

666 to talk to you

667 to get new shoes

668 to know about it

669 to drink something cold

Guess it!

1. I want to go home

2. I want to drink something cold

3. I want to play a game

Speak Up!

A: 시험이 드디어 끝났어! 너 무슨 계획 있어?

B: **나는 TV를 보고 싶어.** 휴식이 좀 필요해.

A: 재미있는 TV 프로그램이라도 있어?

1. **I want to eat pizza**

A: 나 지금 너무 배고파.

B: 나도. **나는 피자를 먹고 싶어.** 넌 어때?

A: 나 피자 좋아해. 좀 먹자.

2. **I want to get new shoes**

A: 생일 선물로 뭐 갖고 싶어?

B: **나는 새 신발을 갖고 싶어.** 내 신발은 오래
됐어.

A: 좋은 생각이야! 부모님께 네가 뭘 원하는지
말씀드려.

3. **I want to go out and play**

A: 오늘 토요일이야. **나는 나가서 놀고 싶어.**

B: 하지만 비가 많이 오고 있어. 우리는 밖에 나
갈 수 없어.

A: 좋아. 그럼, 대신에 안에서 TV 보자.

Track | 76 I don't want to go alone.

p.34

Fill it!

A. 678   B. 672   C. 675   D. 677   E. 674

F. 670   G. 673   H. 671   I. 676

670 나는 혼자 가고 싶지 않아.

671 나는 오늘 공부하고 싶지 않아.

672 나는 일찍 일어나고 싶지 않아.

673 나는 그것에 대답하고 싶지 않아.

674 나는 너를 귀찮게 하고 싶지 않아.

675 나는 시금치를 먹고 싶지 않아.

676 나는 포기하고 싶지 않아.

677 나는 망치고 싶지 않아.

678 나는 너랑 말다툼하고 싶지 않아.

Study words & chunks!

670 to go alone

671 to study

672 to wake up early

673 to answer that

674 to bother you

675 to eat spinach

676 to give up

677 to mess up

678 to argue with you

Guess it!

1. I don't want to eat spinach

2. I don't want to wake up early

3. I don't want to give up

Speak Up!

> **보기**
> A: 나는 오늘 공부하고 싶지 않아.
> B: 왜?
> A: 토요일이잖아. 주말은 나가서 놀기 위한 거야!

1. I don't want to go alone
A: 너 그 애 생일파티에 갈 거야?
B: 난 아직 확실하지 않아.
A: 너 가야 해. **나는 혼자 가고 싶지 않아.**

2. I don't want to answer that
A: 네 휴대폰 비밀번호 뭐야?
B: **나는 대답하고 싶지 않아.** 그건 내 비밀이야!
A: 알았어. 그럼 물어보지 않을게.

3. I don't want to mess up
A: 네가 너의 조의 조장이 되었네.
B: 맞아. 나는 최선을 다할 거야. **나는 망치고 싶지 않아.**

Track | 77 I wanted to win the game.

p.38

Fill it!

A. 686 B. 680 C. 681 D. 683 E. 685
F. 679 G. 684 H. 687 I. 682

> **해석**
> 679 나는 미안하다고 말하고 싶었어.
> 680 나는 멋있게 보이고 싶었어.
> 681 나는 저것을 사고 싶었어.
> 682 나는 경기에서 이기고 싶었어.
> 683 나는 잠들고 싶었어.
> 684 나는 영화 보러 가고 싶었어.
> 685 나는 너에게 그것에 대해 말하고 싶었어.
> 686 나는 너에게 무언가를 물어보고 싶었어.
> 687 나는 너와 친해지고 싶었어.

Study words & chunks!

679 to say sorry
680 to look cool
681 to buy that
682 to win the game
683 to go to sleep
684 to go to the movies
685 to tell you about it
686 to ask you something
687 to be friends with you

Guess it!

1. I wanted to win the game
2. I wanted to buy that
3. I wanted to go to sleep

Speak Up!

> **보기**
> A: 너는 왜 모자를 거꾸로 쓰고 있어?
> B: **나는 멋있게 보이고 싶었어.**
> A: 하지만 전혀 멋있어 보이지 않아! 모자 벗어!

1. I wanted to go to the movies
A: **나는 영화를 보러 가고 싶었어.** 근데 우린 대신 쇼핑하러 갔어.
B: 왜?
A: 우리 오빠가 새 축구화를 사야 했거든.

2. I wanted to ask you something
A: 너 어젯밤에 나한테 전화했어?
B: 응, 했어. **나는 너에게 뭔가 물어보고 싶었어.**
A: 무엇에 관한 거였는데?

3. I wanted to tell you about it
A: 오늘 우리 반에 전학생이 온대.
B: 맞아. **나는 너에게 그것에 대해 말하고 싶었는데,** 네가 어제 일찍 갔어.

Track | 78 I like to travel.

Fill it!

A. 691   B. 692   C. 689   D. 696   E. 694
F. 690   G. 695   H. 693   I. 688

> 해석
>
> 688 나는 여행하는 것을 좋아해.
> 689 나는 집에 있는 것을 좋아해.
> 690 나는 운동하는 것을 좋아해.
> 691 나는 사진 찍는 것을 좋아해.
> 692 나는 TV 쇼 보는 것을 좋아해.
> 693 나는 무서운 이야기를 듣는 것을 좋아해.
> 694 나는 새로운 것을 배우는 것을 좋아해.
> 695 나는 친구들과 이야기하는 것을 좋아해.
> 696 나는 친구들과 시간을 보내는 것을 좋아해.

Study words & chunks!

688 to travel
689 to stay home
690 to play sports
691 to take pictures
692 to watch TV shows
693 to hear scary stories
694 to learn new things
695 to talk with my friends
696 to hang out with my friends

Guess it!

1. I like to take pictures
2. I like to stay home
3. I like to travel

Speak Up!

> 보기
>
> A: 나 어제 중국어 배우기 시작했어.
> B: 너 수영도 배우고 있잖아. 피곤하지 않아?
> A: 전혀 그렇지 않아. 나는 배우는 것이 즐거워. **나는 새로운 것을 배우는 것을 좋아해.**

1. I like to hear scary stories
   A: 너 그거 알아? 나 귀신 봤어!
   B: 정말? 그것에 대해 더 얘기해줘! **나는 무서운 이야기 듣는 거 좋아해.**

2. I like to watch TV shows
   A: 너는 집에서 뭐 하는 것을 좋아해?
   B: **나는 TV 쇼 보는 것을 좋아해.**
   A: 나도 그래. 나는 모든 주말 TV 쇼를 좋아해.

3. I like to play sports
   A: 너는 학교 끝나고 뭐해?
   B: **나는 운동하는 것을 좋아해.** 나는 보통 친구들과 축구나 농구를 해.
   A: 나도 그래. 나는 특히 야구를 좋아해.

Track | 79 I need to talk to you.

Fill it!

A. 697   B. 699   C. 702   D. 705   E. 698
F. 700   G. 703   H. 701   I. 704

> 해석
>
> 697 나는 서둘러야 해.
> 698 나는 너에게 이야기해야 해.
>   (→너한테 할 말이 있어.)

699 나는 엄마께 전화해야 해.
700 나는 화장실에 가야 해.
701 나는 손을 씻어야 해.
702 나는 침착해야 해.
703 나는 좋은 성적을 받아야 해.
704 나는 학교 갈 준비를 해야 해.
705 나는 너에게 질문해야 해.
     (→너한테 물어볼 것이 있어.)

Study words & Chunks!

697 to hurry   698 to talk to you

699 to call my mom

700 to go to the bathroom

701 to wash my hands

702 to stay calm

703 to get a good grade

704 to get ready for school

705 to ask you a question

Guess it!

1. I need to hurry

2. I need to wash my hands

3. I need to get ready for school

Speak Up!

보기

A: 벌써 여섯 시야! 우리 집에서 저녁 먹고 가는 게 어때?

B: 모르겠어. 나는 **엄마께 전화해야 해.** 엄마가 나를 기다리고 계셔.

---

1. **I need to get a good grade**

   A: 나는 좋은 성적을 받아야 해.

   B: 왜? 너 항상 성적 잘 받잖아.

   A: 이번엔 만점을 받을 거야. 그럼, 아빠가 자전거를 사 주실 거야.

2. **I need to go to the bathroom**

   A: 괜찮아? 너 아파 보여.

   B: 아... 나 배가 너무 아파. **화장실에 가야겠어.**

   A: 그래야겠네. 바로 저쪽에 화장실이 있어.

3. **I need to stay calm**

   A: 선생님이 곧 우승자를 뽑으실 거야.

   B: 맞아. **나는 침착해야 하는데,** 너무 긴장돼! 나 정말 우승자가 되고 싶어.

   A: 긴장하지 마. 네가 우승할 거라고 확신해!

Track | 80   I tried to call you.   p.50

Fill it!

A. 713   B. 711   C. 709   D. 706   E. 712

F. 710   G. 708   H. 707   I. 714

해석

706 나는 친절하려고 했어.

707 나는 너한테 전화하려고 했어.

708 나는 최선을 다하려고 노력했어.

709 나는 내 숙제를 끝내려고 했어.

710 나는 문제를 해결하려고 노력했어.

711 나는 내 친구를 격려하려고 노력했어.
    (→나는 내 친구를 기운 나게 해주려고 했어.)

712 나는 잠들려고 노력했어.

713 나는 참으려고 노력했어.

714 나는 컴퓨터 게임을 덜 하려고 노력했어.

Study words & Chunks!

706 to be nice   707 to call you

708 to do my best

709 to finish my homework

710 to solve the problem

711 to cheer up my friend

712 to fall asleep

713 to be patient

714 to play less computer games

Guess it!

1. I tried to play less computer games

2. I tried to fall asleep

3. I tried to do my best

보기

A: 나는 내 친구를 기운 나게 해주려고 했어.

B: 그 애한테 무슨 일이 있었어?

A: 자전거를 타다가 다리가 부러졌어. 그 애는 지금 병원에 있어.

1. I tried to be nice

A: 너는 왜 저 남자애에게 심술궂어?

B: 나는 친절하려고 했어. 근데 그 애가 나를 놀렸어.

A: 아마 너랑 친해지고 싶은 걸 거야.

2. I tried to be patient

A: 나는 참으려고 했지만, 너무 배고파! 더 이상 못 기다리겠어.

B: 진정해. 이제 거의 우리 차례야. 곧 점심을 먹을 거야.

3. I tried to call you

A: 너 어제 안 왔더라. 무슨 일 있었어?

B: 나는 너한테 전화하려고 했어. 근데 휴대폰을 잃어버렸어.

Track | 81 I'm supposed to clean my room. p.54

Fill it!

A. 716 B. 720 C. 715 D. 721 E. 717
F. 722 G. 719 H. 718 I. 723

해석

715 나는 엄마를 도와드려야 해.

716 나는 친구들을 만나기로 되어 있어.

717 나는 내 방을 청소해야 해.

718 나는 지금 집에 있어야 해!
(→나는 지금 집에 가야 해!)

719 나는 아홉 시까지 교실에 있어야 해.
(→나는 아홉 시까지 교실에 가야 해.)

720 나는 열 시까지 잠자리에 들어야 해.

721 나는 규칙을 따라야 해.

722 나는 내 여동생을 돌봐야 해.

723 나는 책임을 맡아야 해.

Study words & chunks!

715 help my mom

716 meet my friends

717 clean my room   718 be home

719 be in class   720 go to bed

721 follow the rules

722 take care of my sister

723 be in charge

Guess it!

1. I'm supposed to be in class

2. I'm supposed to help my mom

3. I'm supposed to be in charge

Speak Up!

보기

A: 나는 내 여동생을 돌봐야 해.

B: 어떻게 동생을 돌보는데?

A: 나는 매일 아침 그 애를 교실에 바래다줘.

1. I'm supposed to meet my friends

A: 너 오늘 무슨 계획 있어?

B: 나는 친구들을 만나기로 되어 있어. 우리는 영화를 볼 거야.

2. I'm supposed to clean my room

A: 너 어디 가고 있어?

B: 나는 내 방을 청소해야 해. 엉망진창이거든.

A: 우리 엄마도 지저분한 내 방에 대해 불평하셔.

3. I'm supposed to go to bed

A: 너는 몇 시에 잠들어?

B: 나는 열 시까지 잠자리에 들어야 해. 하지만 오늘은 늦게까지 안 자고 싶어.

Track | 82 It's time to get ready.

p.58

Fill it!

A. 726 B. 729 C. 730 D. 732 E. 725
F. 731 G. 724 H. 728 I. 727

해석
724 일어날 시간이야.
725 준비할 시간이야.
726 떠날 시간이야.
727 재미있게 놀 시간이야!
728 우리 교실을 청소할 시간이야.
729 음악실에 갈 시간이야.
730 셔틀버스에 탈 시간이야.
731 끝낼 시간이야.
732 결정할 시간이야.

Study words & chunks!

724 wake up　　　725 get ready
726 leave　　　　727 have fun
728 clean our classroom
729 go to the music room
730 get on the shuttle bus
731 wrap up
732 make a decision

Guess it!

1. It's time to get on the shuttle bus
2. It's time to clean our classroom
3. It's time to make a decision

Speak Up!

보기
A: 끝낼 시간이야.
B: 벌써? 하지만 난 아직 안 끝났어. 시간을 좀 더 줘.
A: 그럴 수 없어. 선생님이 기다리고 계셔.

1. It's time to go to the music room
   A: 음악실에 갈 시간이야.
   B: 좋아! 나는 음악 수업이 좋아. 가자.
   A: 기다려. 네 교과서 챙기는 거 잊지 마!

2. it's time to get ready
   A: 나 경주 때문에 긴장돼! 곧 우리 차례야.
   B: 응, **준비할 시간이야.** 긴장하지 마. 우리 이 경주 이길 수 있어!

3. It's time to have fun
   A: 재미있게 놀 시간이야!
   B: 응. 우리 드디어 조별 숙제를 끝냈어.
   A: 야호! 이제 우리 놀 수 있다!

Track | 83 Do you know how to do it?

p.62

Fill it!

A. 740 B. 737 C. 734 D. 733 E. 735
F. 741 G. 739 H. 738 I. 736

해석
733 너는 수영할 줄 알아?
734 너는 그것을 할 줄 알아?
735 너는 그것을 사용할 줄 알아?
736 너는 그것을 고치는 법을 알아?
737 너는 스케이트를 탈 줄 알아?
738 너는 연을 날리는 법을 알아?

739 너는 그곳에 가는 법을 알아?
　　(→너는 그곳에 어떻게 가는지 알아?)
740 너는 그것을 다운로드할 줄 알아?
741 너는 그 문제를 푸는 법을 알아?

Study words & chunks!

733 swim　　　　734 do it
735 use it　　　　736 fix it
737 skate　　　　738 fly a kite
739 get there　　740 download it

741 solve the problem

Guess it!

1. Do you know how to skate
2. Do you know how to fly a kite
3. Do you know how to solve the problem

Speak Up!

보기

A: 이건 우리 엄마의 새 커피 메이커야.
B: 너는 그것을 사용할 줄 알아?
A: 물론 모르지. 나는 커피를 안 마시거든. 우리 엄마만 아셔.

1. **Do you know how to do it**
   A: 나는 이 단계를 깰 수 없어. **너는 할 줄 알아?**
   B: 먼저, 너는 많은 골드가 필요해. 그다음에 새로운 아이템을 사야 해.

2. **Do you know how to fix it**
   A: 네 장난감 헬리콥터가 고장 났어. **너는 그것을 고치는 법을 알아?**
   B: 아니, 근데 우리 아빠는 아셔. 오늘 밤에 내가 여쭤볼게.

3. **Do you know how to get there**
   A: 나 어제 우리 언니랑 같이 새로운 도서관에 갔었어.
   B: **너는 그곳에 어떻게 가는지 알아?**
   A: 7번 버스를 타. 여기에서부터 정류장 세 개만 가면 돼.

Track | 84   I don't know what to say.

p.66

Fill it!

A. 743   B. 746   C. 749   D. 742   E. 747
F. 744   G. 745   H. 748   I. 750

해석

742 나는 다음에 무엇을 해야 할지 모르겠어.
743 나는 무엇을 말해야 할지 모르겠어.
744 나는 무엇을 입어야 할지 모르겠어.
745 나는 무엇을 믿어야 할지 모르겠어.
746 나는 무엇을 골라야 할지 모르겠어.
747 나는 그에게 뭐라고 말해야 할지 모르겠어.
748 나는 무엇을 주문해야 할지 모르겠어.
749 나는 무엇에 대해 써야 할지 모르겠어.
750 나는 그녀에게 선물로 무엇을 줘야 할지 모르겠어.

Study words & chunks!

742 do   743 say
744 wear   745 believe
746 pick   747 tell him
748 order   749 write about
750 get her as a gift

Guess it!

1. I don't know what to do
2. I don't know what to pick
3. I don't know what to wear

Speak Up!

보기

A: 내가 그 애 작품을 망쳤어. **나는 그에게 뭐라고 말해야 할지 모르겠어.**
B: 너는 그 애한테 설명하고 미안하다고 말해야 해. 그 애는 너를 이해해 줄 거야.

1. **I don't know what to get her as a gift**
   A: 내일 엄마 생신이야. **나는 엄마께 선물로 무엇을 드려야 할지 모르겠어.**
   B: 꽃을 드리는 건 어때? 우리 엄마는 꽃을 좋아하시던데.
   A: 좋은 생각이야.

2. **I don't know what to order**
   (I don't know what to pick도 가능)
   A: 나는 무엇을 주문해야 할지 모르겠어[나는 무엇을 골라야 할지 모르겠어]. 메뉴가 정말 많아.

B: 빨리 골라. 사람들이 줄을 서서 기다리고 있어.

A: 알겠어. 시간이 좀 더 필요해.

3. I don't know what to write about

A: 글 쓰는 거 시작했어?

B: 아직 안 했어. **나는 무엇에 대해 써야 할지 모르겠어.**

A: 네가 가장 좋아하는 것들에 대해 쓰는 건 어때?

Track | **85** He seems to be busy.

Fill it!

A. 758 B. 755 C. 756 D. 752 E. 757
F. 753 G. 751 H. 759 I. 754

해석

751 그는 바쁜 것 같아.
752 그녀는 똑똑한 것 같아.
753 그녀는 정말 착한 것 같아.
754 그녀는 정말 인기가 많은 것 같아.
755 그녀는 도움이 필요한 것 같아.
756 그는 너에게 관심이 있는 것 같아.
757 그녀는 남자친구가 있는 것 같아.
758 그는 기분이 안 좋은 것 같아.
759 그는 재미있게 놀고 있는 것 같아.

Study words & chunks!

751 to be busy   752 to be smart
753 to be so nice
754 to be so popular
755 to need help
756 to care about you
757 to have a boyfriend
758 to be in a bad mood
759 to be having fun

Guess it!

1. He seems to be having fun
2. She seems to have a boyfriend
3. She seems to be smart

Speak Up!

보기

A: 그 남자애 저기 있어! 지금 그 애한테 얘기해봐.

B: 난 잘 모르겠어. **그 애는 바쁜 것 같아.**

A: 아니, 그런 것 같지 않아. 그냥 가방을 싸고 있는 거야.

1. He seems to be in a bad mood

A: 그 애 기분이 안 좋은 것 같아.

B: 맞아. 심지어 오늘 아침에 나한테 인사도 안 했어.

A: 그 애한테 무슨 일이 있어?

2. She seems to need help

A: 그 애는 도움이 필요한 것 같아. 다친 것 같아.

B: 너 확실해? 그곳에 그냥 앉아 있는 거잖아.

A: 그 애 무릎 위에 상처 안 보여?

3. He seems to care about you

A: 그 남자애가 너에게 관심이 있는 것 같아. 아마도 그 애가 너를 좋아하나 봐!

B: 절대 아니야! 그냥 가끔 나를 도와줄 뿐이야. 그게 다야.

A: 하지만 그 애는 절대 다른 사람을 그렇게 도와주지 않아.

Track | 86 You look tired.

p.74

Fill it!

A. 764 B. 767 C. 768 D. 765 E. 760
F. 763 G. 761 H. 766 I. 762

> **해석**
>
> **760** 너는 행복해 보여.
> **761** 너는 멋져 보여.
> **762** 너는 화가 나 보여.
> **763** 너는 피곤해 보여.
> **764** 너는 지루해 보여.
> **765** 너는 신이 나 보여.
> **766** 너는 걱정스러워 보여.
> **767** 너는 놀란 것처럼 보여.
> (→너 놀란 것 같아.)
> **768** 너는 혼란스러워 보여.

Study words & chunks!

760 happy   761 great
762 angry   763 tired
764 bored   765 excited
766 worried   767 surprised
768 confused

Guess it!

1. You look confused
2. You look surprised
3. You look tired

Speak Up!

> **보기**
>
> **A:** 너 **지루해 보여**. 뭐 읽고 있어?
> **B:** 이건 역사책이야. 이 책이 나를 졸리게 만들어.
> **A:** 그럼, 그 대신에 뭔가 더 재밌는 거 하자!

1. **You look great**
   A: 너 **멋져 보여**. 그 스웨터 색이 너한테 정말 잘 어울리네. 그거 새 옷이야?
   B: 응. 할머니가 사 주셨어.

2. **You look worried**
   A: 너 **걱정스러워 보여**. 무슨 일이야?
   B: 엄마 반지를 잃어버렸어. 나는 그걸 찾을 수가 없어.
   A: 저런! 내가 그걸 찾도록 널 도와줄게.

3. **You look angry**
   A: 너는 **화가 나 보여**. 무슨 일이야?
   B: 누군가 내 필통을 훔쳐 갔어. 누군지 알아낼 거야!

Track | 87 I feel better.

p.78

Fill it!

A. 772 B. 769 C. 770 D. 776 E. 777
F. 774 G. 773 H. 771 I. 775

> **해석**
>
> **769** 나는 슬퍼.
> **770** 나는 아파. (→나는 몸이 안 좋아.)
> **771** 나는 추워.
> **772** 나는 (몸이[기분이]) 나아졌어.
> **773** 나는 자랑스러워.
> **774** 나는 무서워.
> **775** 나는 긴장돼.
> **776** 나는 편안해.
> **777** 나는 창피해.

Study words & chunks!

769 sad   770 sick
771 chilly   772 better
773 proud   774 scared

775 nervous   776 comfortable
777 embarrassed

Guess it!

1. I feel sad
2. I feel embarrassed
3. I feel proud

Speak Up!

A: 너 괜찮아?
B: **나 긴장돼.** 나 실수하면 어쩌지?
A: 그것에 대해 걱정하지 마. 아무도 알아채지 못할 거야.

1. I feel sick
   A: 나가서 놀자. 나 지루해.
   B: 그럴 수 없을 것 같아. **나는 몸이 안 좋아.** 그냥 여기 있자.

2. I feel better
   A: 너 오늘 몸 상태 어때? 어제 감기에 걸렸었잖아.
   B: **나는 몸이 나아졌어.** 어제 약을 먹었거든.

3. I feel scared
   A: 저 귀신 좀 봐! 나 무서워.
   B: 걱정하지 마. 이건 그냥 영화일 뿐이야.

Track | 88   I got hungry.   p.82

Fill it!

A. 786   B. 783   C. 785   D. 779   E. 780
F. 782   G. 784   H. 778   I. 781

해석

778 나는 배고파졌어.
779 나는 몹시 화가 났어.
780 나는 다 젖었어.
781 나는 운이 좋았어.
782 나는 긴장됐어.
783 나는 다쳤어.
784 나는 어지러워졌어.
785 나는 차멀미가 났어.
786 나는 햇볕에 심하게 탔어.

Study words & Chunks!

778 hungry   779 mad
780 all wet   781 lucky
782 nervous   783 hurt
784 dizzy   785 carsick
786 sunburned

Guess it!

1. I got carsick
2. I got sunburned
3. I got dizzy

Speak Up!

A: 너는 왜 감자 칩을 다 먹었어?
B: 미안해. **나 배고파졌거든.**
A: 내가 나중을 위해 아끼고 있었단 말이야!

1. I got all wet
   A: 너 옷이 왜 이렇게 됐어?
   B: 바람에 우산이 뒤집혔어. **나는 다 젖었어.**

2. I got lucky
   A: 너 또 이 게임 신기록 세웠어?
   B: 응, **나는 운이 좋았어.** 너 게임 더 할래?
   A: 아니, 별로. 여기서 그만할래.

3. I got nervous
   A: 너 왜 병원에서 울었어?
   B: **나는 긴장됐어.** 나는 주사를 무서워하거든.

Track | 89 I'm getting bored.

p.86

Fill it!

A. 788 B. 791 C. 795 D. 787 E. 794
F. 792 G. 789 H. 793 I. 790

해석

787 나는 점점 배고파지고 있어.
788 나는 점점 배불러지고 있어.
789 나는 점점 추워지고 있어.
790 나는 점점 키가 더 커지고 있어.
791 나는 점점 지루해지고 있어.
792 나는 점점 긴장되고 있어.
793 나는 점점 헷갈리고 있어.
794 나는 점점 그것을 더 잘하고 있어.
　　(→나는 점점 더 실력이 좋아지고 있어.)
795 나는 점점 기다리는 것에 지쳐가고 있어.

Study words & chunks!

787 hungry　　　　788 full
789 cold　　　　　790 taller
791 bored　　　　 792 nervous
793 confused　　　 794 better at it
795 tired of waiting

Guess it!

1. I'm getting hungry
2. I'm getting taller
3. I'm getting full

Speak Up!

보기

A: 이 놀이기구 줄이 정말 길어.
B: 언제 우리 차례가 오는 거야? **나는 점점 기다리기 지쳐가고 있어.**
A: 우리는 30분 더 기다려야 해.

1. **I'm getting confused**
   A: 우리 어느 버스를 타야 하는 거야? 10번 아니면 11번?
   B: 내 생각에는 10번 버스… 기다려봐. **점점 헷갈리고 있어.**
   A: 저쪽에 있는 버스 노선도를 확인해보자.

2. **I'm getting better at it**
   A: 너 요즘에도 학교 끝나고 수영하러 다녀?
   B: 응, **나는 점점 더 실력이 좋아지고 있어.** 이번 여름에 바다에서 수영하고 싶어.
   A: 정말 멋지다.

3. **I'm getting bored**
   A: **나는 점점 지루해지고 있어.** 이 야구 경기는 정말 지루해!
   B: 벌써? 근데 게임은 방금 시작했는데!
   A: 나는 야구를 별로 좋아하지 않아. 우리 다른 것 봐도 돼?

Track | 90 She seems so busy.

p.90

Fill it!

A. 797 B. 799 C. 801 D. 804 E. 802
F. 803 G. 800 H. 798 I. 796

해석

796 그는 아픈 것 같아.
797 그녀는 똑똑한 것 같아.
798 그녀는 매우 바쁜 것 같아.

799 그녀는 매우 확신하는 것처럼 보여.
800 그는 오늘 달라 보여.
801 그는 친절한 것 같아.
802 그는 이상해 보여.
803 그녀는 엄격한 것 같아.
804 그는 너에게 관심이 있는 것 같아.

Study words & chunks!

796 sick   797 smart
798 so busy   799 so sure
800 different   801 friendly
802 strange   803 strict
804 interested in you

Guess it!

1. He seems strange
2. He seems sick
3. She seems so busy

Speak Up!

보기

A: **그는 너에게 관심이 있는 것 같아.** 아마
널 좋아하는 것 같아.

B: 왜 그렇게 말하는 거야?

A: 그 애가 수업 중에 너를 계속 쳐다봤어.
그리고 그 애는 너에게만 친절하게 행동
하잖아.

1. He seems different
   A: 그는 오늘 **달라 보여.**
   B: 응, 맞아. 그 애 머리 잘났나?
   A: 그런 것 같아.

2. He seems friendly
   A: 여기서 사진 찍자!
   B: 그래! 우리 사진 찍어달라고 누구한테 부탁
   하자.
   A: 저 사람에게 물어보자. **그는 친절해 보여.**

3. She seems strict
   A: 저분이 너의 새로운 담임 선생님이셔? **저분
   은 엄격하신 것 같아.**
   B: 응. 우리는 모두 8시 30분까지 교실에 와야
   해. 지각한 학생들은 숙제를 더 많이 받아.

Track | 91 It looks like an answer.   p.94

Fill it!

A. 811 B. 807 C. 806 D. 813 E. 809
F. 812 G. 805 H. 810 I. 808

해석

805 그것은 정답인 것 같아.
806 그것은 거미 같아 보여.
807 엉망진창인 것 같아!
808 그것은 재미있는 게임 같아 보여.
809 그것은 어려운 문제 같아 보여.
810 정말 재미있을 것 같아!
811 그것은 진짜 같아 보여.
812 그것은 재미있는 책 같아 보여.
813 방문하기 좋은 장소 같아 보여.

Study words & chunks!

805 an answer   806 a spider
807 a mess   808 a fun game

809 a difficult question
810 a lot of fun
811 a real one
812 an interesting book
813 a nice place to visit

Guess it!

1. It looks like an answer
2. It looks like an interesting book
3. It looks like a spider

Speak Up!

보기

A: 너 뭐(무슨 게임) 하고 있어? **그건 재미있
는 게임 같아 보여.**

B: 응, 이거 정말 재밌어. 난 이것을 내 생일
이라 받았어. 한번 해 볼래?

1. It looks like a real one

  A: 이 사과 네가 그렸어? **그건 진짜 같아 보여.**

  B: 고마워. 나는 실제 사물을 그리는 것을 좋아해.

2. It looks like a mess

  A: 네 방 좀 봐. **엉망진창인 거 같아!**

  B: 그건 또 우리 개가 그런 거야. 우리 개는 항상 어지럽혀.

  A: 같이 청소하자. 내가 널 도와줄게.

3. it looks like a difficult question

  A: 너 3번 답 나왔어?

  B: 나 아직 안 해 봤어. 하지만 **그건 어려운 문제 같아 보여.**

  A: 응, 맞아. 나는 정답을 맞히지 못했어.

Track **71** p.2

Master words & chunks!

(순서 상관없음)

feeling sick, 아픈 것
feeling a little sleepy, 조금 졸린 것
loving the singer, 그 가수를 정말 좋아하는 것
doing my homework, 내 숙제를 하는 것
reading it, 그것을 읽는 것
worrying about the test, 시험에 대해 걱정하는 것
learning English, 영어를 배우는 것
taking after-school classes, 방과 후 수업을 듣는 것
taking an interest in football, 축구에 흥미를 갖는 것

Master sentences!

I started

1 reading it
2 worrying about the test
3 learning English
4 loving the singer
5 feeling a little sleepy
6 taking after-school classes
7 doing my homework
8 feeling sick
9 taking an interest in football

Track **72** p.4

Master words & chunks!

(순서 상관없음)

to understand, 이해하는 것
to calm down, 진정하는 것
to get upset, 화가 나는 것
to get bored, 지루해지는 것
to feel ill, 아픈 것
to feel nervous, 긴장하는 것
to sweat, 땀을 흘리는 것
to wonder why, 왜인지 궁금해하는 것
to regret my decision, 내 결정을 후회하는 것

Master sentences!

I began

1 to understand
2 to feel nervous
3 to get upset
4 to feel ill
5 to regret my decision
6 to sweat
7 to get bored
8 to wonder why
9 to calm down

Track **73** p.6

Master words & chunks!

(순서 상관없음)

talking about that, 그것에 대해 이야기하는 것
asking me questions, 나에게 질문들을 하는 것
being so picky, 까다롭게 구는 것
making that noise, 시끄럽게 하는 것
arguing, 다투는 것
complaining, 불평하는 것
bothering me, 나를 귀찮게 하는 것
fooling around, 장난치는 것
blaming yourself, 너 자신을 탓하는 것

Master sentences!

Stop

1 asking me questions
2 arguing
3 blaming yourself
4 being so picky
5 bothering me
6 talking about that
7 complaining
8 fooling around
9 making that noise

Track **74** p.8

Master words & chunks!

(순서 상관없음)

standing there, 그곳에 서 있는 것
waiting for you, 너를 기다리는 것
making mistakes, 실수들을 하는 것
playing, 노는 것
practicing soccer, 축구를 연습하는 것
dozing off, 꾸벅꾸벅 조는 것
yawning, 하품하는 것
thinking about the problem, 그 문제에 대해 생각하는 것
laughing at his jokes, 그의 농담에 웃는 것

Master sentences!

I kept

1 waiting for you
2 standing there
3 making mistakes
4 yawning
5 laughing at his jokes
6 dozing off
7 thinking about the problem

We kept

8 playing
9 practicing soccer

Track 75
p.10

Master words & chunks!

(순서 상관없음)

to eat pizza, 피자 먹기
to go home, 집에 가기
to watch TV, TV 보기
to play a game, 게임 하기
to go out and play, 나가서 놀기
to talk to you, 너에게 이야기하기
to get new shoes, 새 신발 갖기
to know about it, 그것에 대해 알기
to drink something cold, 시원한 것 마시기

Master sentences!

I want

1 to go home
2 to eat pizza
3 to play a game
4 to watch TV
5 to drink something cold
6 to know about it
7 to go out and play
8 to get new shoes
9 to talk to you

Track 76
p.12

Master words & chunks!

(순서 상관없음)

to go alone, 혼자 가기
to study, 공부하기
to wake up early, 일찍 일어나기
to answer that, 그것에 대답하기
to bother you, 너를 귀찮게 하기
to eat spinach, 시금치를 먹기
to give up, 포기하기
to mess up, 망치기
to argue with you, 너와 말다툼하기

Master sentences!

I don't want

1 to wake up early
2 to go alone
3 to mess up
4 to study
5 to bother you
6 to give up
7 to answer that
8 to argue with you
9 to eat spinach

Track 77
p.14

Master words & chunks!

(순서 상관없음)

to say sorry, 미안하다고 말하기, 사과하기
to look cool, 멋있게 보이기
to buy that, 저것을 사기

to win the game, 경기에서 이기기
to go to sleep, 잠들기
to go to the movies, 영화 보러 가기
to tell you about it, 너에게 그것에 대해 말하기
to ask you something, 너에게 무언가를 물어보기
to be friends with you, 너와 친해지기, 너와 친구가 되기

Master sentences!

I wanted

1 to buy that
2 to go to the movies
3 to ask you something
4 to look cool
5 to say sorry
6 to tell you about it
7 to be friends with you
8 to go to sleep
9 to win the game

Track 78 p.16

Master words & chunks!

(순서 상관없음)
to travel, 여행하는 것
to stay home, 집에 머무는 것
to play sports, 운동하는 것
to take pictures, 사진 찍는 것
to watch TV shows, TV 쇼 보는 것
to hear scary stories, 무서운 이야기를 듣는 것
to learn new things, 새로운 것들을 배우는 것
to talk with my friends, 내 친구들과 이야기하는 것
to hang out with my friends, 내 친구들과 시간을 보내는 것

Master sentences!

I like

1 to hear scary stories
2 to travel

3 to talk with my friends
4 to learn new things
5 to stay home
6 to take pictures
7 to hang out with my friends
8 to watch TV shows
9 to play sports

Track 79 p.18

Master words & chunks!

(순서 상관없음)
to hurry, 서두르는 것
to talk to you, 너에게 이야기하는 것
to call my mom, 엄마께 전화하는 것
to go to the bathroom, 화장실 가는 것
to wash my hands, 내 손을 씻는 것
to stay calm, 침착하는 것
to get a good grade, 좋은 성적을 받는 것
to get ready for school, 학교 갈 준비를 하는 것
to ask you a question, 너에게 질문하는 것

Master sentences!

I need

1 to ask you a question
2 to wash my hands
3 to talk to you
4 to get ready for school
5 to call my mom
6 to go to the bathroom
7 to stay calm
8 to get a good grade
9 to hurry

Track 80 p.20

Master words & chunks!

(순서 상관없음)
to be nice, 친절한 것
to call you, 너에게 전화하는 것
to do my best, 내가 최선을 다하는 것
to finish my homework, 내 숙제를 끝내

는 것
to solve the problem, 문제를 해결하는 것
to cheer up my friend, 내 친구를 격려하는 것
to fall asleep, 잠드는 것
to be patient, 참을성 있는 것
to play less computer games, 컴퓨터 게임을 덜 하는 것

Master sentences!

I tried

1 to cheer up my friend
2 to call you
3 to be patient
4 to fall asleep
5 to do my best
6 to be nice
7 to finish my homework
8 to solve the problem
9 to play less computer games

Track 81
p.22

Master words & chunks!

(순서 상관없음)
help my mom, 엄마를 돕다
meet my friends, 내 친구들을 만나다
clean my room, 내 방을 청소하다
be home, 집에 있다
be in class, 교실에 있다
go to bed, 잠자리에 들다
follow the rules, 규칙들을 따르다
take care of my sister, 내 여동생을 돌보다
be in charge, 책임을 맡다

Master sentences!

I'm supposed to

1 go to bed
2 meet my friends
3 be home
4 help my mom
5 clean my room
6 be in charge
7 be in class

8 take care of my sister
9 follow the rules

Track 82
p.24

Master words & chunks!

(순서 상관없음)
wake up, 일어나다
get ready, 준비하다
leave, 떠나다
have fun, 재미있게 놀다
clean our classroom, 우리 교실을 청소하다
go to the music room, 음악실에 가다
get on the shuttle bus, 셔틀버스에 타다
wrap up, 끝내다
make a decision, 결정하다

Master sentences!

It's time to

1 wake up
2 have fun
3 get ready
4 make a decision
5 leave
6 wrap up
7 get on the shuttle bus
8 clean our classroom
9 go to the music room

Track 83
p.26

Master words & chunks!

(순서 상관없음)
swim, 수영하다
do it, 그것을 하다
use it, 그것을 사용하다
fix it, 그것을 고치다
skate, 스케이트를 타다
fly a kite, 연을 날리다
get there, 그곳에 도착하다, 그곳에 가다
download it, 그것을 다운로드하다
solve the problem, 그 문제를 풀다

Master sentences!

Do you know how to

1 use it
2 skate
3 fly a kite
4 get there
5 solve the problem
6 do it
7 swim
8 download it
9 fix it

Track **84**

p.28

Master words & chunks!

(정답 순서대로)

do
고르다
order
write about
tell him
말하다
입다
believe
get her as a gift

Master sentences!

I don't know what to

1 tell him
2 order
3 pick
4 write about
5 do
6 say
7 believe
8 wear
9 get her as a gift

Track **85**

p.30

Master words & chunks!

(순서 상관없음)

to be busy, 바쁜 것
to be smart, 똑똑한 것
to be so nice, 정말 착한 것
to be so popular, 정말 인기가 많은 것
to need help, 도움이 필요한 것
to care about you, 너에게 관심을 가지는 것
to have a boyfriend, 남자친구가 있는 것
to be in a bad mood, 기분이 나쁜[안 좋은] 것
to be having fun, 재미있게 놀고 있는 것

Master sentences!

He seems

1 to care about you
2 to be busy
3 to be having fun
4 to be in a bad mood

She seems

5 to be so nice
6 to have a boyfriend
7 to be smart
8 to need help
9 to be so popular

Track **86**

p.32

Master words & chunks!

(정답 순서대로)

놀란
bored
great
happy
worried
confused
화난
tired
excited

Master sentences!

You look

1 tired
2 worried

3 happy
4 angry
5 bored
6 confused
7 surprised
8 excited
9 great

Track **87**

p.34

Master words & chunks!

(정답 순서대로)
무서운
better
comfortable
sad
proud
nervous
창피한
chilly
아픈

Master sentences!

I feel

1 proud
2 better
3 sad
4 sick
5 nervous
6 scared
7 chilly
8 comfortable
9 embarrassed

Track **88**

p.36

Master words & chunks!

(정답 순서대로)
dizzy
hurt
all wet
차멀미를 하는
sunburned

mad
배고픈
lucky
nervous

Master sentences!

I got

1 nervous
2 all wet
3 hurt
4 carsick
5 mad
6 hungry
7 sunburned
8 lucky
9 dizzy

Track **89**

p.38

Master words & chunks!

(정답 순서대로)
taller
nervous
confused
better at it
hungry
cold
배부른
기다리는 것에 지친
bored

Master sentences!

I'm getting

1 full
2 taller
3 tired of waiting
4 confused
5 cold
6 nervous
7 bored
8 hungry
9 better at it

Track 90

p.40

Master words & chunks!

(정답 순서대로)

interested in you
sick
strict
이상한
friendly
똑똑한
so sure
different
so busy

Master sentences!

He seems

1 different
2 sick
3 strange
4 friendly
5 interested in you

She seems

6 so busy
7 so sure
8 strict
9 smart

Track 91

p.42

Master words & chunks!

(정답 순서대로)

a mess
a lot of fun
an answer
a real one
an interesting book
a nice place to visit
거미
재미있는 게임
a difficult question

Master sentences!

It looks like

1 a lot of fun
2 a difficult question
3 a spider
4 an interesting book
5 a fun game
6 a real one
7 an answer
8 a nice place to visit
9 a mess

memo ✎

memo ✍

memo ✍